Luxury talent management

Luxury talent management

Leading and managing a luxury brand

Michel Gutsatz
and
Gilles Auguste

palgrave
macmillan

First published 2013 by
PALGRAVE MACMILLAN

Palgrave Macmillan in the UK is an imprint of Macmillan Publishers Limited, registered in England, company number 785998, of Houndmills, Basingstoke, Hampshire RG21 6XS.

Palgrave Macmillan in the US is a division of St Martin's Press LLC, 175 Fifth Avenue, New York, NY 10010.

Palgrave Macmillan is the global academic imprint of the above companies and has companies and representatives throughout the world.

Palgrave® and Macmillan® are registered trademarks in the United States, the United Kingdom, Europe and other countries.

ISBN: 978–1–137–27066–5 hardback

This book is printed on paper suitable for recycling and made from fully managed and sustained forest sources. Logging, pulping and manufacturing processes are expected to conform to the environmental regulations of the country of origin.

A catalogue record for this book is available from the British Library.

Library of Congress Cataloging-in-Publication Data

Gutsatz, Michel.
   Luxury talent management : leading and managing a luxury brand / by Michel Gutsatz and Gilles Auguste.
      pages cm
      ISBN 978–1–137–27066–5
      1. Luxury goods industry. 2. Luxuries – Marketing. 3. Product management.
   I. Auguste, Gilles. II. Title.

HD9999.L852G87 2013
658.8'27—dc23   2012045717

10 9 8 7 6 5 4 3 2 1
22 21 20 19 18 17 16 15 14 13

Printed and bound in Great Britain by
CPI Antony Rowe, Chippenham and Eastbourne

CONTENTS

Lists of insights

List of case studies

List of figures

We appreciate the time and insights of those who contributed to this book. Particular thanks to:

The support of Claire Beaume-Brizzi, whose numerous interviews and written portraits helped get this book published.

The hard work of Pepita Diamand, who helped clarify our perspectives on the luxury industry and contributed valuably to the book's final draft.

The creativity and design of Nicolas Thulie, as reflected in all the boxes, figures and tables that illustrate the book.

The support of our publisher, Eleanor Davey Corrigan, whose patience and good advice made this project fly.

Stuart Crainer, who published our first paper in the *Business Strategy Review* (the London Business School's management journal).

Michel Chevalier, who has since the beginning been very supportive of this work.

Finally, thanks to all the people who helped us enormously by sharing their professional experiences and who prefer that their names remain undisclosed.

	Yes	No
Are you comfortable with ambiguity?		
Can you accept the fact you don't have control over the final product?		
Would you function well in an environment without detailed job description?		
Are you ready to drive the vision of a creator and to partner with him/her?		
Do you believe that it is necessary to operate locally to understand luxury consumers?		

If you answered **yes** to each of these questions, your chance of succeeding in the luxury industry is pretty high!

If you answered **no** to just one of these questions, **be glad you found this book**.

Gilles Auguste conducts strategic and global talent assignments for clients in the luxury and retail industries working with world renowned luxury brands. He is currently Senior Adviser at Sociovision, an independent consulting agency specializing in the monitoring of socio-cultural change. Gilles was formerly VP in the leadership consulting practice at AT Kearney Search and served as International Human Resources Director at Cartier (Richemont Group). Previously, Gilles spent eight years in the consulting industry with Bossard Consultants then Gemini Consulting, as Senior Manager, working on change management issues for a wide range of industries. Gilles is also a teacher at the Catholic University of Paris and with Luxury Group Academy. He received his Master in Human Resources from the Institut de Gestion Sociale in Paris and is a graduate of the Accelerated Development Programme from the London Business School.

Michel Gutsatz is an international expert in luxury brand management and is Director of MBAs at Euromed Management (Marseille & Shanghai) and Adjunct Professor at CEIBS (Shanghai). He advises investment funds, luxury brands, and retailers in Europe, China, and the United States. Prior to that Michel was Managing Director at White Spirit, an Image Strategy Agency. He served as Human Resources and Internal Communication Director of the Bally Group in Switzerland, as a member of the Executive Committee, and here he redeveloped the whole HR function and redesigned the Bally in-store service strategy, convinced that service and retail are critical to the success of a luxury brand. Michel developed the MBA in international luxury brand management at ESSEC Business School. His blog, BrandWatch (michelgutsatz.com), is an acclaimed reference in brand strategy. He is the author (with Michel Chevalier) of *Luxury Retail Management – How the World's Top Brands Provide Quality product & Service Support* (2012).

The global luxury market doubled in ten years: It went from 77 billion € in 1995 to 147 billion € in 2005. Since then it has grown a further 30 percent to 191 billion € in 2011 (Source: Bain: Luxury Goods Worldwide Market Study, October 2011). This impressive development is largely thanks to a generation of talented luxury executives who *professionalized* the industry – an industry made up of less than 200 brands – transforming regional companies into global players.

This fascinating business now faces four talent issues that will shape its future:

1. ***Preparing for Succession.*** The generation that led this major development is close to retirement and the industry will have to find new talent to replace them (see Figure 4.1 Exemplary leaders of the luxury industry – milestones). Critical questions like "Do we hire talent from outside or inside the industry?" have to be answered.

2. ***Managing Luxury's Idiosyncrasies.*** The luxury industry has three major characteristics that its executives know well:

   • Most brands are part of family businesses and have to be managed as such (never forget that both LVMH and Richemont, luxury's two top groups, are family businesses – respectively, the Arnault and the Rupert families).
   • Creation is critical to its success – the management of creative teams and designers is a profession in itself that requires specific managerial skills.
   • Retail is a very important challenge because the store is where the brand meets its customers: luxury brands moved into this field only in the last ten years and face important

issues there: hiring store managers, developing sales experts, building compensation systems, building long lasting customer relationships, etc.

3. ***Strengthening the Customer Experience.*** Luxury customers' behaviors have evolved: They now seek more than just the product; they expect an *experience* and a personalized relationship. They look for a level of service that goes way beyond the standards luxury brands deliver today. This will require new competencies and innovative approaches to retail and marketing in order to gain customer loyalty.

4. ***Readiness for the Asian Markets.*** The luxury industry is entering new markets that will be the levers of its future growth: Identifying local talent and mastering cultural issues are critical. This is a major concern for China, which will become luxury's no. 2 market within the next decade. As the Bain & Company analysts say: *"Go East! What's in your luggage?"*.

Such "people change" issues are generally tackled intuitively, mainly based on experience: Many executives will reference their previous experiences– mostly in marketing, finance or distribution – when making decisions. They often lack expertise in what the future holds: creation, retail, the internet and customer experience. They master the intricacies of the business but lack a conceptual vision of what luxury is about, its unique business model and the very specific competencies and behaviors that are needed to grow within it. All luxury brands are full of both success stories and extraordinary failures due to the insufficient personal adjustment of another wise talented executive who did not adapt to the industry (if coming from the exterior) or to a new brand (if coming from the inside).

Luxury brand executives also often rely on the external expertise of consulting companies and headhunters to tackle what is fundamentally a mix of change management issues with a very strong *people* dimension. Although they may have significant experience of the industry, these experts are themselves faced with a major organizational challenge: few of them master both the change management and people issues.

Our view is that luxury brands will have to address each of these four challenges in an innovative manner, based on two major factors:

- The unique aptitudes and skills cultivated by the generation of executives that led the luxury industry to its present heights need to be understood and transferred. A major study led by one of the authors has already achieved much of this: In 2000, most of the CEOs and executives of the luxury industry were interviewed, and their unique competencies and Leadership Profiles identified.
- "Talent Management" has to be seen as critical to all business decisions made within the shifting global landscape and these turbulent times. Those brands that are ready to adopt a new mindset about their "Talent" and can foster specific leadership skills will emerge as future winners in the luxury industry.

This book has four objectives:

To provide a concrete and comprehensive framework of what Talent in the Luxury Industry is about	**To assert our strong beliefs regarding leadership challenges** that change this industry and the consequences for people
To illustrate through real life examples & case studies the distinctive cultural value, management style, and specific integration process for each population working for this industry	**To offer a "Resource Book" for any manager, creator, or executive** seeking to develop and/or to maintain career momentum in this particular industry

Louis Cartier, grandson of the founder, revolutionized timepieces when he introduced the Tank watch in 1917 (Photo Atelier Nadar, courtesy Cartier)

PART 1

Understanding the fundamentals of the luxury industry

We are not here to sell boilers and vats,
but for the potentiality of growing rich beyond the dreams
of avarice.

Samuel Johnson, while auctioning off
the contents of a brewery, 1781

Introduction

The objective of Part 1 is to give a unique understanding of what the luxury industry is about and what differentiates it from other brand-centered industries.

This understanding is critical to anyone wanting to lead a successful career in luxury: The hurdles are numerous, and even efficient executives from other industries have been known to fail because they had underestimated these idiosyncrasies.

We have identified 17 topics that summarize what makes luxury such a different industry:

- Two unique factors:
  - The family business heritage
  - The essence of creation
- Three business characteristics
  - The luxury business model in Six key points
  - Four unique financial features
  - The time factor

- One conceptual framework
- Three organizational models
  - The traditional French Craft Organizational Model
  - The Flexible Network Organization: the Italian variant
  - The Flexible Network Organization: the American variant
- Four corporate cultures
  - Tribal
  - Mechanist
  - Holistic
  - Mercenary
- Four key populations to manage
  - Manufacture/Workshop workforce
  - Creatives and designers
  - Retail staff
  - Executives/Managers

1.1 Two unique factors

1.1.1 Unique factor 1: The family business heritage

Time is a critical factor for the understanding of luxury.

A fundamental dimension of time is of essence to a luxury brand: **Heritage**.

- The brand's history is proof of its power and ability to survive. It becomes a trusted reference for customers in a chaotic and uncertain world.
- The customers' capacity to appreciate luxury is something that cannot be acquired overnight. Valuing luxury craftsmanship, brand history, etc. are elements that customers learn with time. A perfect example is found in the development of special exhibitions (like Louis Vuitton's Retrospective Exhibition in Shanghai in 2010) or artisan shows in new major markets like China. Such activities are necessary to embed the luxury culture in these new markets.

- The essence of quality is durability: a luxury product is generally made to last a long time and may even, in some cases, be transferred to the next generation. This is the selling argument of some major watch brands, such as Patek Philippe who advertises, *"You never actually own a Patek Philippe. You merely look after it for the next generation."*

Heritage means that brand awareness is built over relatively long periods of time, which helps explain the role that **Families** have played in this industry. Figure 1.1 (the genealogical tree of the

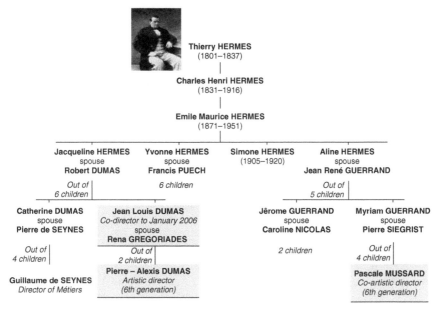

Figure 1.1 The genealogical tree of the Hermès family (simplified)

They are also working in the Family Group: Laurent Momméja (grandson of Francis Puech), CEO of Castille Investment (tableware products), and two sisters of Pascale Mussard: Hermine Redele, Internal Manager, and Maria Schaefer, Product Manager. A special person is artist Philippe Dumas (brother of Jean-Louis) who, as an artist, is the creator of all the drawings that can be found on their website and in all Hermès communication.

In May 2012, Hermès announced that the current CEO, Patrick Thomas, would retire within two years and that Axel Dumas, 46, nephew of Jean Louis Dumas, (and currently responsible for the distribution network in France) would replace him as CEO. With his cousin Pierre-Alexis, Creative Director, the sixth generation is now in place.

Source: Adapted from different sources: La Tribune / Hermès Annual Reports.

Hermès family over six generations) gives a perfect example of this.

For these reasons, people who want to work in the luxury industry need to prove and master the capacity to cope with brand history, the continuity of the brand's creator, the specific family management culture and other peculiarities inherent in a family business.

Coping with brand history

To become iconic, luxury brands must survive their original creator and may need decades to be significantly imprinted in the customers' mind. A considerable number of today's luxury brands are more than 150 years old and continue to be nurtured and grow – carefully balancing tradition and modernity. However, this depends on the original category of the brand.

As illustrated in Figure 1.2 (below), the oldest luxury brands are watch and jewellery brands, all established before 1850. The

	Apparel		Leather Accessories		Watches & Jewelry		Others	
2000								
	VERSACE	1978						
	G ARMANI	1974						
	YSL	1962						
1950	GIVENCHY	1952						
	DIOR	1946					ESTEE LAUDER	1946
			FERRAGAMO	1920			LANCOME	1935
1900			GUCCI	1922				
	CHANEL	1910	PRADA	1913	ROLEX	1908		
					VAN CLEEF & ARPELS	1906	MONTBLANC	1906
					BULGARI	1884		
1850	BURBERRY	1856	LOUIS VUITTON	1854	BOUCHERON	1858		
					CARTIER	1847	CHRISTOFLE	1848
					PATEK PHILIPPE	1845		
			HERMES	1837	TIFFANY	1837		
					JAEGER LECOULTRE	1833	GUERLAIN	1828
1800								
					BREGUET	1775		

Figure 1.2   Creation dates of major luxury brands

accessories brands (leather goods, writing instruments, etc.) were mostly established in the early twentieth century (except Hermès and Louis Vuitton). Apparel brands are a different story: Those that still exist were set up after 1950 (with the exception of Chanel and Burberry). Achieving luxury status needs the consistent building of a durable brand image; only time will tell if a brand will make it.

We can also look at the heritage of luxury brands from a different perspective by considering their graphic codes and visual identities (see Fig 1.2.a below). **Respecting the brand history and heritage is akin to respecting history: a brand manager is also a keeper of tradition – and when that tradition bears the name of the owners of the brand, the challenge is mighty.**

Brand	Graphic Code	Year Introduced
HERMÈS	The Orange Box	1945
CARTIER	The Cartier logo has existed as such since the beginning of the twentieth century and has only ever been slightly modernized	Early twentieth century
BULGARI	The Bulgari logo in Roman letters first appeared in signage for the Via Condotti store	1933[1]
TIFFANY	The Blue Box	1837[2]
PRADA	The Savoy coat of arms and Savoy figure-of-eight knots have been an integral part of the Prada brand ever since Prada was awarded the patent "Fornitore Ufficiale della Real Casa Italiana"	1919

Figure 1.2.a   Origin of the graphic codes of some luxury brands

Insight: Companies live and die – luxury brands survive

The Heritage issue can be seen in a different light too. Take the Dow Jones. Of the 12 original companies listed in the first Dow Jones Industrial Average in 1896, only one still exists as it originally was: General Electric. All the others have either disappeared or have been bought and merged into larger companies. Companies are born, live, develop and die. But in the luxury industry to achieve icon status the brands must survive their creator and be in existence for over 50 years to significantly imprint on the mind of customers.

Exhibit: What's become of the 12 original DJIA companies?[3]

Company	What Became of It
American Cotton Oil Distant	Ancestor of Best foods
American Sugar	Evolved into Amstar Holdings
American Tobacco	Broken up in 1911 antitrust action
Chicago Gas	Absorbed by Peoples Gas, 1897
Distilling & Cattle Feeding Whiskey Trust	Evolved into Millennium Chemical
General Electric	Going strong and still in the DJIA
Laclede Gas Active	Removed from DJIA in 1899
National Lead Today's NL Industries	Removed from DJIA in 1916
North American Utility	Combine broken up in 1940s
Tennessee Coal & Iron	Absorbed by US Steel in 1907
US Leather (preferred)	Dissolved in 1952
US Rubber	Became Uniroyal, now part of Michelin

Insights into the family business system

Figure 1.3 shows that most major luxury groups, whether they are still held by the original creator's family or owned and managed by newcomers, are indeed Family Businesses.

Three groups constitute the basis of the family business system: the **Business** (including managers & employees), the **Ownership** of the business and the **Family** that has control of the business. Although memberships of these three groups generally overlap, they each have their distinctions.

The critical point that must never be overlooked is that a *family* should not be managed and governed like a business – and vice

	Generations from Original Founder	New Family Owners
BULGARI*	Paolo Bulgari, Chairman – 3rd generation Francesco Trapani, CEO – 4th generation	
HERMES	Alexis Dumas, Artistic Director – 6th generation	
ESTEE LAUDER	Leonard Lauder, Chairman Emeritus – 2nd generation William P Lauder, Executive Chairman – 3rd generation Aerin Lauder, Artistic Director – 3rd generation	
FERRAGAMO	Ferrucio Ferragamo, CEO – 2nd generation	
LVMH		Bernard Arnault, Group CEO – Founder of LVMH Delphine Arnault, VP Christian Dior Couture – 2nd generation Antoine Arnault, Com Dir Louis Vuitton – 2nd generation
PRADA	Miuccia Prada, Designer – 3rd generation	
PPR		Francois Pinault, Chairman – Founder of PPR Francois Henri Pinault, Group President – 2nd generation
RICHEMONT		Johan Rupert, Group Chairman – 2nd generation
RIEDEL	Georg Joseph Riedel, Chairman – 10th generation Maximilian Joseph Riedel, CEO USA – 11th generation	

Figure 1.3   Who manages which brand?

* Part of LVMH Group since the end of 2010.

versa. As we shall see in a case study in Part 2, more than a few executives have lost their standing for having overlooked this fundamental aspect. At the same time, because the needs, goals and memberships of the three circles are intertwined and inter-dependent, the management and governance of these three groups must be carefully coordinated (see Figure 1.4).

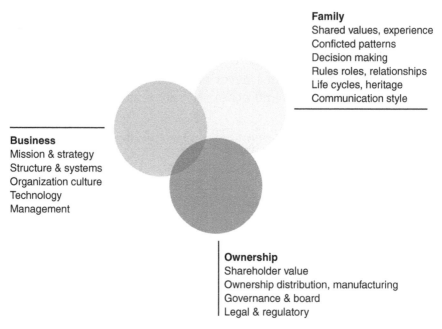

Family
Shared values, experience
Conficted patterns
Decision making
Rules roles, relationships
Life cycles, heritage
Communication style

Business
Mission & strategy
Structure & systems
Organization culture
Technology
Management

Ownership
Shareholder value
Ownership distribution, manufacturing
Governance & board
Legal & regulatory

Figure 1.4   The model of luxury family businesses

A clear understanding of how this Family Business model works will help those who share critical decision with family members – for whom business, family and ownership circles could overlap – anticipate certain issues endemic to family businesses.

The following are five critical areas in which such issues may arise. For each of them we have identified key questions that a manager should ask him/herself:

1. **Capital:** How are the brand's financial resources allocated among different business and family demands?

2. **Control:** Who has decision-making power in the family and the brand? Is the board of directors the real decision maker or does the owner make decisions?
3. **Careers:** How are individuals selected for senior leadership and governance positions in the brand or family? Is family membership an overriding factor, a consideration or a disqualification? Can family in-laws be included?
4. **Conflict:** Can the family stop discordant human relationships spilling over into the business system? If two family members have a disagreement about compensation, for example, can they attend a family social event without fighting?
5. **Culture:** What values are critical to the family and business systems and how are these values transmitted? Does business performance influence the power of individual family members?

The case of luxury groups: the family's leadership role and its value to the business

Figure 1.5 provides some key insights to the three main Family Luxury Groups and the strategic assets they bring to their brands.

	Rupert Family (Richemont Group)	Pinault Family (PPR Luxury Division)	Arnault Family (LVMH)
Representative companies	Cartier, Montblanc, Van Cleef & Arpels...	Gucci, YSL, Boucheron ...	Louis Vuitton, Dior...
Family's leadership style	"Overview & Control"	"Learning & Trust"	"Vision & Hands-On"
Likely family contributions	Financial resources Industry expertise C-level recruitment Creation Committee member	Financial resources Industry expertise Foster M/A deals C-level recruitment Portfolio of brands management	Financial resources Industry expertise C-level talent and designer recruitment Access to pools world class talent

Figure 1.5   What strategic asset does the family bring to the business?

Case 1: The Rupert touch: "overview and control"
Johan Rupert has a very active participation in the Creative Product and Communication Committee (which oversees and controls product launches and the communication of each brand).

He finances and leads the strategic acquisitions that nurture Richemont's portfolio of luxury brands. Recent acquisitions he led include: Roger Dubuis watch workshop, Azzedine Alaia Haute Couture, Ralph Lauren watches (licence) and the e-business Net-A-Porter.

He has a permanent *"overview"* of the way the executive board manages their luxury brands, and when the Group or one of the brands undergoes a critical period (such as a major acquisition, a key leader departure, etc.), he personally *"controls"* the management and the communication of that brand.

Case 2: The Pinault touch: "learning and trust"
François-Henri Pinault, who took over as Chairman from his father François Pinault in 2005, makes a very different contribution:

He was instrumental in the recruitment (in 2004) of a great leader from outside the Luxury Industry to lead and manage the Gucci Group (see Robert Polet Case Study in Part 2).

He attracts "young" leaders and Artistic Directors from well-known Luxury Brands and *"trusts"* them to fill critical positions and key responsibilities within the Gucci Group organization – like Valérie Hermann (formerly CEO of John Galliano) moving to YSL, Isabelle Guichot (formerly CEO of Van Cleef and Arpels) moving to Balenciaga and Fridda Gianini who became Creative Director at Gucci.

He treads very carefully when managing brand portfolio development: both *"learning"* the specific characteristics of the luxury industry and considering the weight of the historic brands of the PPR Group in consumer goods and entertainment.

Six years later, having learnt all the intricacies of luxury, he decided on a reorganization through which Robert Polet's position disappeared and he himself took over the direct management of all the brands. *"I wanted to be more in direct contact with the luxury brand managers,"* Mr. Pinault said in an interview to the Wall Street Journal (17 February 2011).

Case 3: The Arnault touch: "vision and hands on"
Bernard Arnault, both the majority owner and creator of the LVMH Group, has a great and powerful ***"vision"*** for the LVMH Group in the luxury industry.

He personally oversees the recruitment and development of key Artistic Directors – and attracts foreign Artistic Directors (like John Galliano at Dior – after a stint at Givenchy – or Marc Jacobs at Louis Vuitton) and French elite executives from outside the luxury industry, when necessary. For years (before Marc Jacobs was recruited), he was sitting at the Louis Vuitton Creative Committee that oversees all product creation.

He was one of the first to have recruited executives from P & G and Unilever, primarily for their marketing competencies, at a time when "marketing" was a word totally unknown to French luxury brands.

Arnaud is very **"hands on"** with each of its luxury brands, and when critical business decisions are to be made, he likes to visit his own boutiques as a mystery shopper, with a great "obsession for details."

His vision of the LVMH Group has led him to a very aggressive and opportunistic brand portfolio expansion (one remembers the Homeric battle of 1999 with PPR over Gucci). His latest significant business acquisitions lead LVMH towards *hotel management* and to a significant minority share in Hermès.

Lessons learned

Lesson 1: There is a time in the lifecycle of heirs where they must prove that they can devise their own way and restructure the Group they inherited.

Lesson 2: You cannot lead luxury groups without – at some point – taking a very "hands on" role, be it by being part of the creative process or by seeking direct relationships with the CEOs of the major brands.

Lesson 3: Developing the Group's brand portfolio through major acquisitions is critical, but a Chairman must be more than a *banquier d'affaires* or merchant bank.

1.1.2　Unique factor 2: The essence of creation

The essence of Luxury is creation: All luxury brands were created by men and women who brought unique creative skills to their clients, often breaking the rules and norms of their times. As Coco Chanel once said: *"Je travaillais pour une société nouvelle. On avait habillé jusque là des femmes inutiles, oisives, des femmes à qui leurs cameristes devaient passer les bras; j'avais désormais une clientèle de femmes actives; une femme active a besoin d'être à l'aise dans sa robe. Il faut pouvoir retrousser ses manches."*[4]

This heritage is still vividly present: The role of the Creative Director, sometimes known as the Art Director, and of the creative team is to uphold this creative flow. Karl Lagerfeld, when he joined Chanel in 1991, brought together all the codes of the Chanel brand, calling them the "instantaneous elements of identification of Chanel – its spiritual patrimony." These include: a black tipped woman's shoe, a quilted bag with its golden chain, the little black dress, a cross-shaped multicolored brooch, the "tailleur Chanel" jacket, a catogan headpiece, a camellia and the golden double C button. These *codes* are materials and shapes the designer and the customer can use to identify the brand through its products.

The original creator (if he/she is still with the company) or the Creative Director are the "guardians of the brand" and its image, while also breathing new life into the brand by creating a permanent flow of new products that drive traffic into the stores.

Luxury brands are about creation and designers: New product design at a luxury brand is a process whose origin is in a designer's head. Whatever the brand, be it with a famous designer, a Creative Director coordinating designers, in-house designers or freelancers, designers are involved. There are two characteristics of luxury brands that other brands do not necessarily have:

- Creation of new products is a top-down process.
- The critical importance of designers in building and developing a luxury brand requires CEOs to have specific managerial skills.

The creation of new products: a top-down process embedded in vision

There are different designer profiles, two of them being noteworthy:

The "Aristocratic Designer": This is a very French profile, although found in most of the countries. She/he is convinced that she/he has something to bring to the world, irrelevant of the world itself. She/he considers her/himself to be a *creator* and as such has not much to do with trivial aspects like functionality, trends, customers, price. With such designers, the process is totally top-down, the designer being only driven by his/her creative vision and aesthetics. Some may even pride themselves in being ignorant of technical matters. Such designers may come to consider themselves as artists: French artists are known for not wishing to let people know where they have been trained, as if their talent was just divine grace.

The "Street-Wise Designer": This a very Anglo-Saxon profile. He/she is very aware of what customers want, of what street styles are, of business constraints and objectives. Of course, each designer will cater to the needs of a different "street" but both their creative vision and business will drive them. They will often have certain technical know-how. The parallel with Anglo-Saxon artists is here also pertinent: They openly discuss their training and acknowledge its importance. Business aspects, like merchandising, are an important part of their training process in London or New York's leading design schools.

Creator / Designer
2 standard profiles

The "Aristocratic designer"	The "Street-Wise designer"
> Very French profile	> Very Anglo-Saxon profile
> "Artists" who believe they have something to bring to the world	> Very aware of customer needs, street styles, business constraints and objectives
> Little to do with functionality, trends, customers needs, price	> Acquired technical skills at international creative schools
> Some have technical skills	> Driven by their creative vision and business imperatives
> Drives a top down process based on his/her creative vision	
> Working in this industry	

Figure 1.6   The two designer profiles

Regardless of the designer's profile, creating a new product for a luxury brand is a process that is embedded in the brand's vision.

Designers identify with the brand: they are intrinsically involved in its vision and values.[5] Creating a new product is therefore a permanent mix of tradition (the brand heritage) and modernity (the capacity of the designers to reflect and shape their times). There is no such thing as testing here. Customers will be taken into consideration only though the sources of inspiration of the designers and their business sense.

Insight: Designers are experts with complex sources of inspiration[6]

Designers need to be viewed as experts in their field: They are part of a very closed group of people that share practices, references, mental representations and behaviors. They are experts in the sense that they have extensive knowledge of their field (garments, shoes, leather goods, watches, jewelry, etc.): They are

→

constantly exposed to enormous amounts of products; they travel extensively visiting fairs, exhibitions, competitors' stores; they read magazines – all of which gives the man encyclopedic knowledge of their field. They will share a common context of remembered designs, of materials used, of shapes, of techniques and of manufacturing that ultimately equate to an expertise. Designers are experts in the sense that their designs are based on long-term memory, on recent experiences, on their current visual field and their current concerns. Their one vital skill is to spot trends and to mentally translate them into products. Their imagination is strictly visual: They see their designs more than they can talk or write about them (sketching is there only to communicate with others).

What Eckert and Stacey say of knitwear design applies to all categories: *"Complexity arises from the interactions between the inherent limitations of knitted structures, material properties, manufacturing constraints, market pressures and aesthetic considerations. Knitwear is created by multidisciplinary teams, and problems arise from failures of communication between team members. The product is highly dependent on the context created by other designs and cultural and technological developments."*[7]

One of the essential aspects of a designer's professional life is the complexity of their time-management constraints. The following table shows that designers have to manage simultaneously between one and three collections, and therefore stretch themselves enormously. The collection that is analyzed here (Autumn–Winter 12, which runs from June 11 to January 12) is broken down in four sub collections:

1. Early (or pre) collection, which has to be in the stores in May 2012: it is the "teaser" for the fall collection.
2. Main collection, to be in the stores between June and August 2012.
3. Cruise collection for Christmas, to be delivered in October 2012.
4. A special Runway collection – linked to the fashion show that takes place in January 2012, which is to be in the stores by early September.

$\rightarrow$

Included in the same period we also must consider an additional collection:

5. The Spring–Summer 12 Runway Collection that reaches the stores in February 2012

Seen from the stores' perspective, the situation is quite simple:

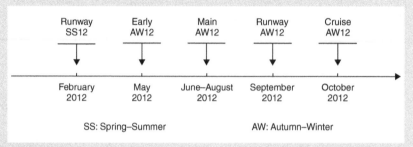

Seen from the designers' and the merchants' perspectives, it is in fact quite complex. There are:

- Four major teams concerned: designers (including developers), merchants (collection planners and buyers), manufacturers, commercials (retailers and wholesalers).
- Eight major tasks to achieve: information gathering, design, collection planning, prototyping, sampling, production, pricing and buying.
- Five collections handled simultaneously (not to mention the different product categories).

A formula for success: a leadership duo of a creator + a businessman

The paradox of a luxury brand is that it needs to engender a strong emotional link with its customers, while at the same time being managed as a very complex business. Business complexities include ensuring the right gross margins, purchasing raw materials at the right prices, choosing distribution channels carefully, opening stores in the best locations of major world cities, with outstanding designs and fixtures and heavy inventories – and dealing with the huge investment required.

For a business to be successful one therefore needs a creator who is in the limelight and a manager working to make it a commercial success. Who, then, is more important? This is where things get tricky. The manager must be able to run the show, but he must remain behind the scene.

Creator and manager therefore a need for very strong relationship based on mutual trust and the understanding that the two roles must be played in harmony.

Creators create the products and develop their vision of the world (or what a woman is... or what beauty is about, etc.) but can a creator also be business-wise? Could a creator develop a business by him/herself? That was clearly the case before the 60s: Christian Dior, Coco Chanel, Charles Christofle, Charles Lewis Tiffany, Louis Vuitton, at different periods in time, managed their companies directly.

But going global and developing a brand necessitates different competencies and skills. Successful brands have seen the emergence of a new *leadership duo* – that of creator and businessman – which unites left-brain management skills and right-brain creative skills as listed in the following graph (see Figure 1.7).

This model is transnational: We've seen it in the USA with Calvin Klein and Barry Schwartz at Calvin Klein; in the UK with Angela Ahrendt and Christopher Bailey at Burberry; in France with Marc Jacobs and Yves Carcelles at Louis Vuitton; in Italy with Miuccia Prada and Patricio Bertelli for Prada, and the mythic duo, Tom Ford and Domenico De Sole at Gucci.

The respective roles of the CEO and Creative Director

Making the brand consistent is the primary role of the Creative Director. Nothing escapes his eye. She/he must apply their vision of **the aesthetics of the brand** to everything:

• Product presence (product lines, materials, design).

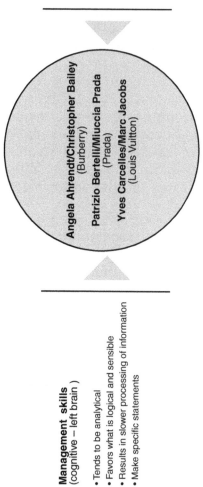

Management skills
(cognitive – left brain)

- Tends to be analytical
- Favors what is logical and sensible
- Results in slower processing of information
- Make specific statements

Creative skills
(emotional – right brain)

- Tends to be intuitive, impressionable
- Favors what feels goods
- Uses metaphors, images narratives
- Results in rapid processing of information
- Make sweeping statements

Angela Ahrendt/Christopher Bailey
(Burberry)

Patrizio Bertelli/Miuccia Prada
(Prada)

Yves Carcelles/Marc Jacobs
(Louis Vuitton)

Leading leadership duo

Figure 1.7   The luxury leadership duo: a formula for success and innovation

- The spatial and retail environment (store design, shopping bags, packaging, office design and furnishings, in-store music, window merchandising).
- The services (the sales method, the after sales service).
- The visual image of the brand (the graphic identity of the brand, including internal templates such as faxes, presentations, letters, memo, emails).
- The communications mix (advertising, events, fashion shows, annual reports, website).
- The people working for the brand (uniforms, employee training, the grooming of the salespersons).

What do all these have in common? They are "key experiential providers."[8] They are what makes the customer *experience* the brand, relate to the brand, feel the brand. When a customer enters the brand's store, the ambience, the layout, the quality of the salesperson's approach, the service provided as well as the products are all unique opportunities for the brand and the customer to forge an emotional relationship and for the brand to create a unique experience the customer will remember. When the customer opens a magazine that depicts one of the brand's ads, when she/he reads about the designer in some other magazine, when she/he is invited by the brand to a special event or sees her/his favorite music star sporting one of the brand's products, the emotion will be enhanced. This is the major reason why the Creative Director is critically important to the development of the brand and its business.

The CEO and the Creative Director both have their areas of expertise and their responsibilities (listed in Figure 1.8).

Brand Vision is what underpins both roles, and their respective responsibilities and every activity must be consistent with it. Many of these topics need concerted decisions (see the Leadership Duo case study in Part 3). This can be examined through the following case study, which looks at how Tom Ford "created" the Creative Director role at Gucci.

CEO & Management team	Creative Director & Design team
Distribution channels	Product presence (product lines, materials, design)
Store locations	
Choice of suppliers	Retail environment (store design, windows, visual merchandising, store music, packaging, shopping bags)
Recruiting store managers and salespeople	
On time delivery of goods	
Gross margin management	Communications (advertising, events, fashion shows, annual reports, website)
Pricing strategy	Brand visuals (logo, graphic image)
General collection structure (if merchandising team exists)	Services (selling attitude, after-sales)
	People (grooming, uniforms)

The (shared) Brand Vision

Figure 1.8   The respective roles of CEO and Creative Director

The Tom Ford case study

Tom Ford, the Creative Director for Gucci from 1995 to 2005, and the template for all Creative Directors, himself says:

I'm one of those people who has a vision. I always know instantly: yes, no, I like it, I hate it. My job is just that all day long, express-ing my vision in some way or another. ... Gucci IS Tom Ford. Of course, Gucci is not all me. It's a part of me. But I have expressed myself.... The New York Studio 54 side of me is more Gucci... (For YSL) it was hard at first. I had to tap into a different side of my personality, a different side of my taste level. Growing up in New Mexico, a lot of what I was exposed to was Hispanic culture, which was lace and ruffles, pattern, color. And that's very much about what Yves Saint Laurent does, to a certain extent.[9]

"I saw that Tom, like me, was a maniac,"[10] says Domenico De Sole, the Gucci Group CEO. Creative Directors are maniacs, they are detail focused: Tom Ford is obsessive about details. He moved a white stool, he worried that the handrail would give shoppers splinters and he set little marks on the stereo volume so the music would provide the proper ambience before the opening of a new

→

YSL store in New York. Tom Ford knew the New York store would set the tone for all YSL stores worldwide.

Tom Ford also has an acute sense of the business: *"I intellectualize to a point, but in a fitting or when I am working on anything, I say okay, but does she look skinny in it? Is she going to feel good? If the answer is no then who cares that's it's about the Russian revolution blah blahblah and the theme is blah blahblah... who CARES*[11]*? When the customer puts on those pants she doesn't care what the original inspiration was. She cares about whether her butt looks good... I worry too much about whether it would sell or if people would like it."*

Tom Ford adds *"I have to give a huge amount of credit to Domenico; he has made it possible for me to work. We are a great team. I completely trust Domenico with my life. Not everybody has that. And the fact of the matter is that I am a business-minded designer. I cannot divorce the commercial from the creative, because my goal is to create something beautiful that people will want more than anything in the world. When they find something they want, they buy it, and if they buy it, it makes sales, and if it makes sales... It's a tangible side of a creative idea that works – money."*[12]

As Carine Roitfeld, the editor of French Vogue and a stylist for Gucci from 1995 to 2000 says, "Tom is artistic, but he has such a strong business side, and that is very rare. For most designers, it's the cut of a jacket. With Tom, it's the cut of the jacket and all the accouterments. He thinks about the car the woman drives, the kind of place she likes to live, how she likes to have sex. Tom considers all these things when he thinks about Gucci or YSL."[13]

The Creative Director is the one person that personifies the vocabulary of the brand AND who knows what will sell. This mix of vision, creative instinct and business instinct is rare. Most designers lack the business instinct and will favor a much more top-down approach, thinking 'this is good for the brand because I have designed it. This is how it should be' – irrelevant of business constraints: who cares if the market wants men's rubber-soled shoes, if I consider that this brand will only have leather-soled

$\rightarrow$

shoes? Why bother with functionalities if the design is great? Why bother with fit if the clothes are made only for anorexics? This is the aristocratic attitude – the "Moi le Roi Soleil" syndrome – which most French couturiers and some British designers exemplify. But ultimately in the twenty-first century luxury brands are about creation AND business and business always has the last word. Customers are the ultimate deciders on which brand meets their needs, their desires and their expectations.

1.2   The three business characteristics of the luxury industry

Based on the authors' in-depth work with numerous luxury brands over the last ten years,[14] we have identified three major characteristics that define the Luxury Industry:

1. The Luxury Business Model in six key points
2. Four Unique Financial Features
3. The Time Factor

In addition to these three business characteristics, other key elements characterize the luxury industry: luxury categories, size of markets and major players (see Figures 1.9 & 1.10).[15]

1.2.1   The luxury business model in six key points

There are many business models in the luxury industry – but they all share a certain number of common qualities. The key six points are:

Point 1: presence

Luxury brands are rather small (with an average annual turnover of around 60 to 100 million euros) yet enjoy *very strong awareness*

	Business size (€ billion)	Key Players
Ready-to-wear	20	Chanel, Dior, Hermès, Louis Vuitton, Armani, Dolce & Gabana, Zegna, Gucci, Burberry, Prada, Salvatore Ferragamo...
Leather goods	15	ST Dupont, Hermès, Longchamp, Coach, Lancel, Dunhill, Montblanc, Gucci...
Fragrances and cosmetics	30	Estée Lauder, L'Oréal, LVMH, Procter & Gamble, Chanel, Coty Prestige, Clarins, Shiseido, Sisley...
Wine & Spirits	80	Diageo, Pernod Ricard, Bacardi, LVMH, Constellation, Remy Cointreau, Brown Forman, Campari, Fortune Brands...
Watches	10	Rolex, Cartier, Omega, Breitling, Jaeger Le Coultre, IWC, Baume et Mercier, Blancpain, Breguet, Patek Philippe...
Jewelry	30	Cartier, Tiffany, Bulgari, Chopard, H Stern, Mikimoto, Graff, Harry Winston, Van Cleef & Arpels...
Tableware	5	Baccarat, Puyforcat, Christofle, Hermès...
Total	190	

Figure 1.9   The luxury industry: major players

1 | The Business Model
> Luxury brands are rather small
> Branding skills are very important
> Both production & distribution are strictly controlled & often subcontracted
> Price ranges are very wide
> Staff numbers are very limited

2 | Financial Characteristics
> Luxury business is a very high break-even business
> Gross margins are very high: 60–70%
> Pricing is critical
> Cash needs are limited

3 | The Time Factor
> Time frames are specfic
> The collection cycle
> Long turn-around times: no short-term impact of major strategic decision

Figure 1.10   The three business characteristics of the luxury industry

among consumers and a worldwide presence. Worldwide presence refers to either of two types:

- **Regional:** A brand strong in its domestic market and one other regional market. Coach is an example that is strong in the US and in Japan.[16]
- **Global:** A brand strong in all major luxury markets (USA, Europe, Japan, China, other Asian markets, etc.). Louis Vuitton, Gucci, Prada, Cartier are global brands.

Point 2: branding

The definition of the brand identity and its control are critical: *Brand management skills are very important in this industry.*

Point 3: production

Production is *strictly controlled* and can either be in-house or, more often, subcontracted.

- Hermès is a perfect example of in-house production with its very diverse "métiers" (silk, porcelain, leather goods, etc.).
- Most Italian leather goods brands (like Gucci, Prada) outsource a large part of their production to skilled "ateliers" in Northern Italy.

Point 4: distribution

Distribution is a mix of retail, wholesale and licensing – the importance of each channel depending on the time in the brand's lifecycle. Sales figures can therefore be very difficult to assess and compare: providing global sales at the consumer level of a given brand is impossible because it needs adding up sales done by very diverse distribution actors.[17]

Point 5: pricing

Luxury brands adopt a very wide price range: The *very high prices* of a number of products are essential to the business model – generating high gross margins and helping build the brand awareness – while lower entry-level price points ensure a wide customer base. The whole development of the luxury industry over the last 20 years has been built on the democratization of luxury – what one of the authors calls "Luxe Populi."[18]

Point 6: staffing

Staff numbers are very limited: The greatest proportion of staff is in the stores – which can represent up to 85/90 percent of the total – whilst staff numbers at headquarters remain relatively small.

1.2.2   Four Unique Financial Features

Feature 1: A luxury business has a very high break-even point

Fixed costs and capital expenditure (CAPEX) are high for a variety of reasons (see Figure 1.11):

- *Retailization*: The requirement to have a worldwide retail presence in prime locations and the importance of flagship stores in major world capitals.
- The strong development of concessions in department stores.
- The exceptional quality of products (at Hermès, it takes a skilled craftsman approximately 18 man-hours to manufacture a single "Kelly Bag").
- *The cost of running unprofitable yet necessary activities*: French fashion brands like Dior, Givenchy or Yves Saint Laurent have impressive Haute Couture activities which legitimizes their existence in the eyes of the media and customers. But the cost is high: The price of a couture fashion show runs between $700,000 and $4.5 million! And two are required per year.

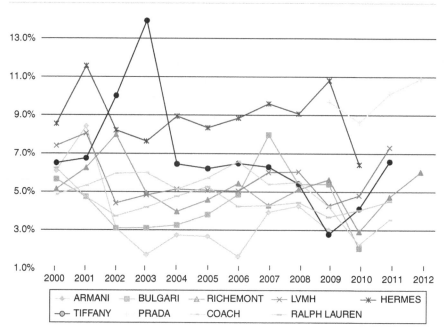

Figure 1.11 Capital expenditure as a % of sales

Source: Annual Reports.

- The costs linked to in-house manufacturing (these costs are inexistent for the American luxury brands that outsource their production like Coach and Ralph Lauren).
- The significant marketing and communications expenses (up to 10–15 percent of annual sales for brands like Bulgari and the Richemont Group) (see Figure 1.12).[19]

Feature 2: Luxury companies garner very high-gross margins

All public luxury companies have gross margins between 60 and 75 percent – and some major brands, whose figures are not publicly available, may reach 80 Percent (Figure 1.13).

Feature 3: Pricing is critical

Pricing is critical to ensure both the exclusivity of the products (exclusive products are priced higher) and the democratization of luxury itself (to democratize luxury, a brand must offer entry point products).

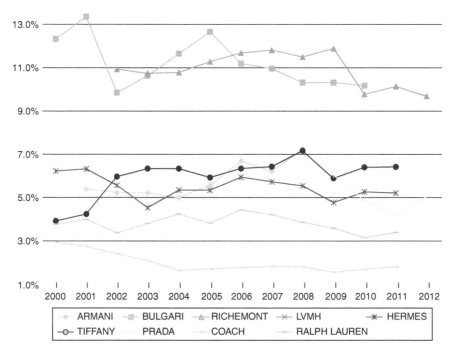

Figure 1.12 Marketing and communication expenses of major luxury groups and brands as a % of sales

Source: Annual Reports.

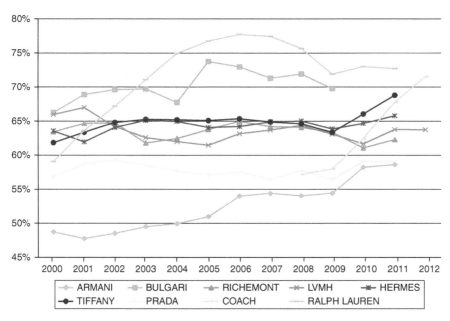

Figure 1.13 Gross margins of major luxury groups and brands

Source: Annual Reports.

Insight: Financing the development of a luxury brand

A very detailed analysis of the luxury industry was published in 1999 by Goldman Sachs: "Branded Consumer Goods: A Global Review." One of their major findings concerns the evolution of *total* capital employed by listed luxury companies over the period 1986–2000. It had been multiplied by ten, when sales were only multiplied by eight. This means that capital employed had grown at a 17.8 percent annual rate against 16 percent for sales. As a consequence the industry's global Net Operating Margin After Tax (NOMAT) has been steadily decreasing.

There are two major reasons for this, both linked to the development strategy that luxury brands had adopted at the time:

1. The push to control distribution, through buy-outs of former distributors and the refurbishment or opening of new stores in prime locations
2. The extension of brands into new product areas.

NOMAT was also impacted by two other phenomena:

1. The money spent on communications strategies to develop and maintain brand awareness
2. The shift in product mix from high margin products to lower margin lifestyle products to attract new customers

Pricing is also critical when it comes to developing new markets, while brand managers must ensure that they have a consistent pricing strategy across all markets.

Luxury brands therefore need talent that have pricing competencies – competencies which are very specific to the industry. Pricing in luxury is more value-based and benchmark-based than cost-based.

Feature 4: Cash needs are quite limited

High margins mean significant profit levels once all fixed costs are covered.

1.2.3 The time factor

Luxury brands evolve within a **specific time frame**: Luxury product launches can take a long time, involving huge investments and delivering payoff only after three to four years. During this period, collections need to be created and manufactured in time for yearly events, fairs or shows, such as biannual fashion shows, Basel Watch Fair or AIHH watch fair. Luxury brands therefore have to manage both short-term issues and long-term investments.

The fashion cycle (for luxury fashion brands): Contrary to fast-fashion, luxury consumers may take a long time before they really perceive – and react to – major changes in styles or brand positioning. and react to it. This applies to most other product categories as well. This means that when brands need to be turned around, **major strategic decisions have no short-term impact.** The most famous example is the Gucci turnaround: Dawn Mello was hired as Creative Director in October 1989; Maurizio Gucci cleaned up the business of its "drugstore image" in 1990 (discontinuing the wholesale business to department stores; slashing duty free; cutting products from 23,000 to 7000; closing stores from 1000 to 180; refurbishing stores); Tom Ford was hired as RTW Designer in September 1990; he became Creative Director in May 1994 and presented his first "solo" collection in October 1994. The jet-set can be said to have "adopted" Gucci in October 1995, and it wasn't until 1996 that things really took off, with sales reaching $880 million (vs. $200 million in 1992) and a 19 percent net margin (vs. loss in 1992, 1993 and break-even in 1994). Altogether, it took five years.[20]

1.3 The luxury brands' conceptual framework

To understand the conceptual framework within which all luxury brands evolve we need to understand the role of *brand meaning* in getting customers to agree to pay a premium for a product – and examine its business consequences.

1.3.1   Brand meaning and the customer's agreement to pay

The luxury industry doesn't just produce goods: it produces *mental frameworks*. Embedded in the actual branded good or service is a representation of what this brand and this good or service means. This representation can be called a Meaning System. When you buy a good or service you also buy the brand's history, the images and words attached to it, the brand's name and what it triggers in you. What makes a luxury good or service so very different from any mass-market commodity (even a branded one) is that the representational dimension (the meaning system) is huge compared to the objective dimension (the good or the service itself). In the luxury segment, sales are not determined by competing functional qualities but rather by symbolic qualities: Do I prefer a Gucci bag or a Hermès bag? One doesn't compare the bags' functionalities (even if they may prove important) – instead one relates to a brand. One brand will satisfy a customer's symbolic and experiential needs more than the other. And the customer is ready to pay for it.

Economists say, "when a customer is ready to pay for a product beyond its total cost, there exists a potential rent. Rent materializes if the price of the product includes this phenomenon. The specificity of luxury is that brand rent is huge."[21]

This is reinforced by the fact that branded luxury goods deal mostly with the customer's body and appearance. These objects are worn (apparel, leather goods, watches, jewelry, perfume & cosmetics, etc.) and are an essential part of how we feel about ourselves or how others perceive us. Others are closely linked to our home (tableware, silverware, interior decoration, etc), and for people given to socializing and entertaining, this is a critical part of the way others perceive who you are. Last but not least, branded luxury goods are popular presents: the price, the quality, the aesthetics of the gift are messages to the recipient about who *the giver* is. In all cases, the person is at stake: s(he) is totally committed in each of these objects.

This **economic model of a luxury brand** is synthesized in Figure 1.14.[22] Figure 1.14 shows that there are a certain number of

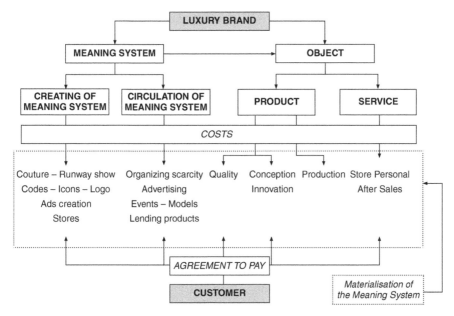

Figure 1.14 The economic model of luxury

costs associated with a luxury brand, costs against which can be plotted the customer's agreement to pay for the emotion, the experience as well as the products:

- Cost of creating the Meaning System (couture and runway costs, codes creation costs, store costs, advertising development costs)
- Cost of circulating the Meaning System (organization of scarcity costs,[23] advertising costs, events costs, models and product lending costs)
- Costs linked to the products (conception & innovation costs, quality costs, production costs)
- Costs linked to the service embedded in the product (store personnel costs, after sales costs)

The challenge facing luxury brands is to maintain an appropriate gap between those costs and the customer's agreement to pay, because this is where the profits are: anything that may cause this gap to shorten or disappear is a threat to the brand.

The bottom part of Figure 1.14 focuses on the contact points that exist between the customers and the brand: all these points are materializations of the Meaning System and all must be consistent with the Meaning System. If not confusion can set into the customer's mind as she/he will perceive critical divergences between the Brand's Meaning System and its materializations.

1.3.2 The brand meaning system and its business consequences

The importance of the Luxury Brand's Meaning System being evident, we need to enter it and understand the overall conceptual framework, which all luxury brands must conform to if they want to find their customers. Not all brands will follow these guidelines unfortunately – but they are necessary to **build what is the ultimate objective for a luxury brand: customer desire.**

This framework (see Figure 1.15) has a three-level structure:

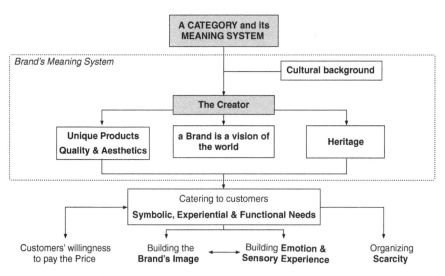

Figure 1.15   The luxury brand conceptual framework

Level 1: A category and its meaning system

Each Brand is rooted in a **category** (Champagne, Beauty, Fashion, Cognac, Watches, etc.).

Consumers share a common perception of this category which drives their attitudes and behaviors before they even have an image of a given brand. For instance, Moët & Chandon's Brand Meaning is embedded and driven by the customer perception of its category, champagne. Champagne has three major dimensions in its perception by consumers. First, it is the drink of "passage" that accompanies all major moments of life, which carry us from one period to another, such as a birth, marriage, retirement, new job or new year. Then, it has a seemingly sacred meaning, with specific serving rituals and specific glasses; it was created by a monk and comes from in the region where the French kings were crowned. Finally, it has a spiritual element with 'magical' virtues (it is a drink that brings people together; it is not drunk for the sake of getting drunk; it makes us 'light' and happy).

Level 2: The brand's Meaning System

The brand builds its own **Meaning System** which is a complex mix of:

- A "founding object" (an ingredient, an object, a promise, a craft, etc.). For instance, Louis Vuitton's founding object is the trunk.
- Its Ethics[24] or "Vision of the world" (delivering benefits the consumers expects or values) – which most of the time refer to its creator's vision.
- The Brand's Codes (its Aesthetics[25]) which include:
  - its logo and its monogram (LV / YSL / the Chanel double C);
  - its brand colour (the Hermès Orange; the Tiffany Blue);
  - its unique signs (the Cartier 'Blue Ball' on its watches or the Roman characters used on their watch dials; the Breguet blue hands; the Chanel camellia);
  - its trademark – a quality guarantee – that says this product has been created by a craftsman (the Veuve Clicquot Anchor;

the Hermès Tilbury; the Patek Philippe 'Croix de Calatrava').
- Iconic products (like the Hermès Kelly Bag; the Gucci Bamboo Bag or loafer).
- Its history and heritage.
- Its cultural background (A French brand has its roots in France whilst an Italian brand will refer its customers to Italy) – meaning that a given brand also includes references to cultural myths.

Level 3: The business consequences

The pricing strategy
If the Brand's Meaning System satisfies the customers' material, symbolic and experiential needs...

... They will be willing to pay a price premium (as we have seen previously)

The product and its quality
The product should deliver simultaneously the technical, functional and emotional benefits consumers seek

... and be of a superior quality. As every global study shows, quality is a hallmark of all luxury brands in the customers' mind.

The brand image: building the emotional link with the customer
Communication should build a consistent brand image over time – and be capable of developing the unique mix that characterises all major luxury brands: the mixture of tradition and modernity.

This brand image is at the service of emotion: the relationship that a brand builds over time with its customers is of an *emotional* nature. In the design of products, in their aesthetics, in the advertising (think of recent campaigns like Cartier's

"Odyssey" or Chrysler's "Made in Detroit" with Eminem and Clint Eastwood), in the use of major artists (for instance when Dior commissioned Chinese artists to "reinvent" traditional Dior codes and create art pieces as they did in 2009) and in the choice of their spokespersons, luxury brands make lavish use of emotion.

In all cases this communication must be consistent with the brand's heritage and Meaning System (see the Case Study: Analyzing the Cartier "Odyssey").

Case study: Analyzing the Cartier "Odyssey"

"An evening of mystery, at 13 rue de la Paix...in the heart of Paris, where the Cartier myth was born. The beginning of a wonderful adventure, a tale of creativity spanning 165 years of history, from the garland style to Art Deco, from the Cartier animal kingdom to tutti frutti jewels, from platforms to mysterious clocks that seem to make time stand still."[26]

Cartier aired in the early months of 2012 a movie "Cartier Odyssey," marking the brand's 165th anniversary. It is a magnificent storytelling of the brand – which we will decode for laymen.

"This film is built on the history of Cartier. It illustrates several fundamental elements of Cartier philosophy, creative vision and more particularly Cartier vision style," said Pierre Rainero Cartier's Image Style and Heritage Director.[27]

Why the panther?
The muse behind the Cartier Odyssey is of course the panther, the emblematic figure of the Maison since the 1930s. Jeanne Toussaint was then Artistic Director and "la Panthère" was her nickname. "She embodied a type of feminine elegance which was very assertive and independent. She was also a true original. In 1948 she was to become the creator of the first figurative panther in Jewelry, a

→

brooch. A panther completed with a very beautiful emerald which would be sold to the Duchess of Windsor."

Why Russia? (chapter 2)
Cartier is the Maison that has served the kings and the queens of this world. Cartier obtained no fewer than 15 different royal warrants in the first 30 years of the twentieth century. This effectively made Cartier the most well-known luxury jeweler among the royal courts of the world.

In the film the panther captivates the Grand Duchess Maria Pavlovna in her sleigh in Saint Petersburg: At the very beginning of twentieth century Pierre Cartier was embraced by Russian aristocracy. "Cartier was the Jeweler of Kings and the King of Jewelers" as the Prince of Wales (the future King Edward VII) pronounced.

Why the dragon? (chapter 4)
"This dragon has a very Cartier look: yellow gold, encrusted with onyx and emerald eyes. These two animals sized each other up as if two influences, two cultures were coming face to face. That the panther should find itself in China alongside the dragon of the Great Wall is no fantasy. It is a symbol of the Maison's universalism ... and of one of its major current market, China."

Why the elephant? (chapter 5)
The Panther then crept into a Mughal-inspired palace in India, a fantastical incarnation of the "Tutti Frutti" style. This famous blend of blue and green that Cartier introduced to the jewelry world is influenced by Islamic faience. Yet in the Western culture this type of color mix was considered bad taste. When Cartier launched this color blend, it became fashionable and was named the "Cartier Style."

India reminds us also that Indian Maharajas were among the most important Cartier clients in the nineteenth and twentieth century.

$\rightarrow$

Why the plane? (chapter 6)
The panther then jumps on a plane, manned by the famous Santos Dumont. In order to have greater control while flying his aircraft, the aviator Alberto Santos Dumont ordered one of the first wristwatches from Cartier in 1904. This watch is still one of the brand's bestsellers.

Why the rings? (chapter 2)
Two classic timeless pieces are in the film: the LOVE bracelet which has captivated us since 1970 and the three-band TRINITY ring that was created in 1924. Both have acquired legendary status and are also bestsellers.

"Cartier Jeweler since 1847"

Louis Vuitton and Takashi Murakami

In 2003 Louis Vuitton embarked on an association with the Japanese artist, Takashi Murakami. The immediate outcome was an extraordinary reinterpretation of a Vuitton design classic. Six years after that, the collaboration continued and had evolved. This case study demonstrates how a luxury brand works with designers to develop a unique mix of tradition and modernity – so as to build a strong emotional link with its customers.

The 2003 collaboration had three essential characteristics:

1. The brand agreed to an interpretation of its logo in colour (contrary to all marketing precepts), temporarily abandoning its traditional Monogram canvas. This aroused the desire of the client who entered the shop attracted by these bags cascading with colour, even though they left having purchased one of the classic bags. (The clients' capacity for transgression often has its limits, but the role of the brand is to make it possible.)

→

2. By collaborating with a contemporary Japanese artist, the brand directly engaged with its No. 1 market, Japan. Further on we see how this has evolved in subsequent partnerships between Murakami and Vuitton.

3. This was a mark of true innovation; not just the initial encounter, but the building of an ongoing relationship between an artist and a contemporary luxury brand. Of course, Louis Vuitton had previously worked with Stephen Sprouse in 2001 (the Tag bag), but this was the first time that an Art Director (Marc Jacobs) relied on a designer whose creative universe fit into that of the brand. The alliance continued with the "Monogram Cerises" collection in 2005, then again in 2008 with the "Monogramouflage," a camouflage print on the Monogram. However, this last collection assumed a new form of collaboration, which in itself is also a real innovation. Late in 2007, during an exhibition of Takashi Murakami's work at the Museum of Contemporary Art in Los Angeles, Louis Vuitton installed a temporary boutique of 80 m2 IN the museum where it sold a limited edition of Murakami designed bags; the "LV Hands Neverfull" collection.

In April 2008 a similar event took place at the Brooklyn Museum: fake "touts" offered the new collection outside the museum where the Murakami retrospective was being held. Thus, the encounter between art, the artist, and the brand reached its culmination by being conducted in a place – the museum – where the exhibition of paintings and the sale of products were united.

The collaboration between Louis Vuitton and Murakami has since taken on another dimension.

In 2003, to accompany the creation of the first collection, Takashi Murakami created a video called "Superflat Monogram" in which a little Japanese girl meets Puti Panda, one of Murakami's characters (who already existed in his work exhibited in 2007): she enters the world of Louis Vuitton, living a real reinterpretation of "Alice in Wonderland."

The intermingling of the world of the artist, the world of the brand and the wonderful imagination that is at the heart of any luxury brand, was total.

$\rightarrow$

In 2010 Takashi Murakami, to celebrate six years of collaboration with the brand, created a new video called "Superflat First Love" where, in a Manga universe, a young Japanese girl meets Gaston Vuitton through a magical chest that allows one to travel through time. Once again the artist created the encounter between the story (of the brand), the fantastical (the magic chest, a symbol found in many stories), the brand (with its iconic chest) and his own universe (Puti Panda and colour Monograms)

The outcome of this saga: The character, Puti Panda – wearing the characteristic Vuitton logo on its ears – was sold in Vuitton stores in the form of cuddly toys and key rings.

We should admire the force and coherence of this ensemble: where any other luxury brand would merely have asked an artist to create a range of products, Louis Vuitton created a universe and prolongs it in the long term. Let's not forget that luxury is time.

1.3.3   Organizing scarcity

The distribution strategy should organize (forms of) scarcity to help build the customers' desire.

For instance, the use of limited editions or of pop-up stores displaying collections that will only be sold during the event are perfect examples of how a luxury brand can organize scarcity.

1.3.4   Building brand consistency throughout the organization

From a business perspective the major objective of a luxury brand is to ensure that its whole organization is consistent with the Brand's Meaning system. Figure 1.16 gives a list of all the critical Contact Points (or interfaces) that the brand should monitor and where the same question should be asked to the employees in charge: Can you deliver this Brand Meaning promise at this given contact point with the customer?

The list of contact points as shown here is not all-inclusive, but it illustrates a major point: Attention to detail is crucial. Store deliveries must be in line and on time with advertising so as not to frustrate customers. Quality control should be a priority so as not to present customers with flawed products in the store. Sales staff should be trained to reflect the brand history and values – and should be experts of the brand and not just there to push sales.

This figure also shows very clearly the respective territories of the Creative Director and CEO and confirms that this duo has a clear responsibility to work hand-in-hand in harmony to develop the business. All instances of disharmonious duos show that they are ultimately not viable and that the brand's performance will be negatively impacted.

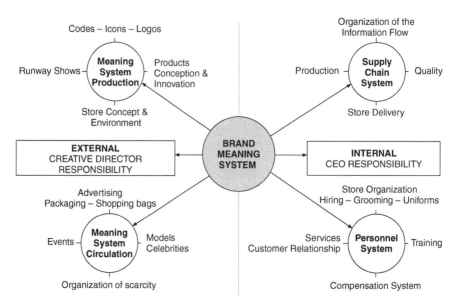

Figure 1.16   Building brand consistency

1.4   The three luxury organizational models

Talent is undoubtedly linked to organization. The organizational model that a brand follows will determine the skills and competencies that it requires. For example, if your production is outsourced you will need quality control inspectors instead of craftsmen. Similarly a brand that decides to be structured like a department store – as Bally did in 1999 – will need to hire merchandisers capable of building a collection. It is therefore vital to understand the different organizational models that luxury brands adopt.

To facilitate the understanding of the how luxury companies are organized, we will refer to and adapt a paper by Marie Laure Djelic and Michel Gutsatz[28] that describes the three main organizational models in luxury (see Figure 1.17), all linked to different countries (France / Italy / USA). These main three models are still dominant, even though new emerging models are now apparent, especially when it comes to the international management of a brand.

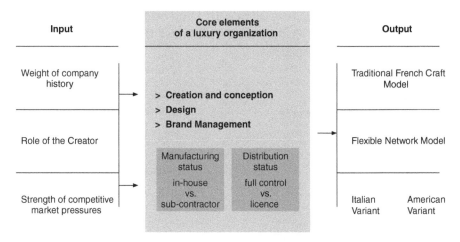

Figure 1.17 Identifying the different luxury organizational models

1.4.1 The traditional French Craft Organizational Model is based on the cult of "The Creator"

The central place of the product and its creator, as the ultimate bearer of value, is strongly asserted.

Manufacturing: These companies (all in fashion, tableware, leather goods) have a long tradition of craftsmanship, where everything has been made in-house and through labor intensive processes – examples are Haute Couture in fashion, Louis Vuitton and Hermès for leather goods and Christofle for tableware.

Organization: One can point to systematic centralization, strong integration of all activities and a hierarchical form of organization and control where the creator has traditionally been at the top. The introduction of traditional managerial functions and roles is a relatively recent phenomenon and managers have often remained in the shadows of the creators. As a consequence marketing is not an essential function in these luxury brands.

Resistance to change: When tradition and the past define best practice to the extent that they do in French fashion, tableware and leather goods companies, changes are bound to be perceived as threats and external influences as a source of disturbance. Faced with increasing turbulence in their market and environment, French fashion companies have first tried to change the world rather than themselves.

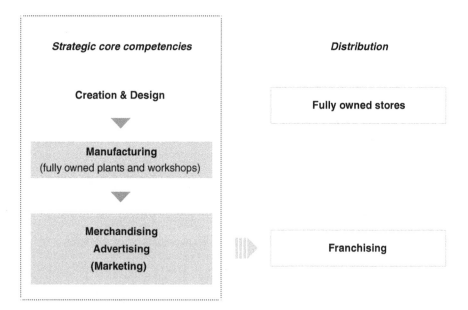

Figure 1.18 The traditional French Craft Organizational Model

This type of strategy and structure aims at bringing the organization under full control by limiting external dependencies and warding off external influence.

1.4.2   The Flexible Network Organization: the Italian variant (including French cosmetics and jewelry)

All that is non-strategic is outsourced

Manufacturing: Italian companies generally set up their manufacturing activity in three tiers

- Key products of their core business are kept in-house – couture apparel for Versace, women's ready to wear and accessories for Trussardi, some of the leather goods for Gucci.
- For the rest of their core business, Italian companies generally subcontract manufacturing to a tight network of industrial partners and craft workshops over which they maintain strict control. This particular type of flexible network fits in nicely with the traditional Italian "industrial district" organization.[29]
- Non-core products – eyewear or perfumes for example – are manufactured by licensees.

Organization: These companies emphasize the management of the brand rather than the management of products. They build upon concepts – those intangible goods that define the brand – using them as a basis for product lines and products as well as communication tools, marketing strategies and even the design of stores. The quest for such overall coherence is ultimately the responsibility of the creator who is not only an artist and a designer but also a brand manager.

Distribution: Italian companies either work through fully owned stores or through a franchise network over which they keep tight control.

While predominant in the Italian luxury goods industry, the 'Italian' model is also characteristic of some non-Italian companies, particularly in jewelry (Cartier or Tiffany's) or in accessories (Coach, ST Dupont, Montblanc or Baume et Mercier).

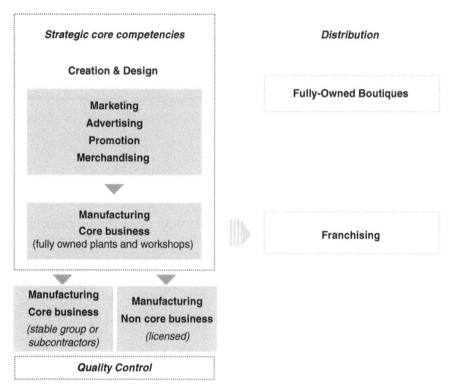

Figure 1.19   The Italian Flexible Network Organization

1.4.3   The Flexible Network Organization: the American variant

Retain only a narrow range of activities in-house, which are defined as strategic or core competencies

Organization: American brands retain only a narrow range of activities in-house, which they have defined as their strategic or core competencies. These may include design, the choice of fabrics and materials, promotion, advertising, merchandising, quality and distribution strategy. In other words, American companies only tend to keep full control of strategic decision making, the conception of the product and overall management of the brand image.

Manufacturing: Is entirely licensed off or, for the core business, subcontracted.

Distribution: In the United States, it is generally through licensees and outlet stores. In foreign countries, American fashion companies tend to distribute through a network of licensees. Some major US luxury brands (like Ralph Lauren), having seen the success of business models developed by French and Italian brands, and have started opening flagship stores of they own – thus moving to develop their own retail network.

A striking example of this flexible network, tending towards the *virtual organization*, is Calvin Klein (when it was owned by Calvin Klein himself) where both manufacturing and distribution had been fully outsourced, and where the core organization had been reduced to creation, public relations, communications, merchandising and control of the brand.

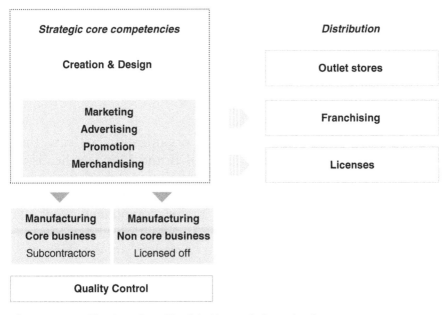

Figure 1.20   The American Flexible Network Organization

1.4.4 The issue of international development

All luxury brands have been developing globally using a common model – by moving from using local distributors to setting up subsidiaries when their growth was sufficient. This led them to move from a simple organization where a Regional Distribution management structure based at headquarters (generally a Wholesale Manager with a team of regional heads) – managed the distributors with the support of central functions (Finance, Communications and PR).

Figure 1.21   Third-party distribution management

Once the subsidiary is set up, its organization reflects the headquarter's organization: A regional Brand Manager heads a team with retail, HR, merchandising, operational marketing and operations. So in a sense, the regional organization mirrors the global organization – with some major components kept at headquarters like strategic marketing and creation, and of course, production, which is kept under strict control in the domestic market.

Some brands have very recently come to understand the importance of regional customer behaviors (especially in cosmetics) and

Figure 1.22 The regional organization, mirror of the global organization

of regional tastes in product design. This has led to a double move:

1. All brands for which "Made in ..." was not a critical component of the brand identity have set up factories in their major markets to minimize costs, such as Coach, or be closer to their customers, as is the case for cosmetics companies like L'Oreal – which has additionally bought local brands to optimize their brand portfolio.
2. Some brands – in order to cater to the local tastes of their customers especially in China, given the size and potential of the market – have decided to take the mirroring of their headquarter's organization to the next step: Prada is setting up a design center in Hong Kong, Burberry and Coach have created strategy teams in China.

1.5 The four luxury corporate cultures

Much too often, newcomers to the luxury industry, being unaware of the subtle environment of a brand, will believe that the brand's corporate culture is embedded into its communication. This is a major mistake.

Each brand has over time developed a unique mix of history, heritage, symbols, roles and storytelling, with generations of leaders who will have left their imprint and vision. This unique mix nurtures *living* corporate cultures that deserves attention.

There are four core elements that are specific to the luxury industry (see Figure 1.23) and that will drive four Luxury Corporate Culture Frameworks:

Core element 1: rituals, signs, symbols
Core element 2: behaviors, customs, attitudes, roles
Core element 3: memories, stories, values, ideas, sense of belonging
Core element 4: ethics and vision of the world

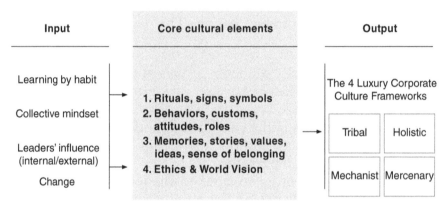

Figure 1.23 The luxury corporate culture framework

Source: Adapted from J.C. Fauvet (2004): L'élan sociodynamique, Editions d'Organisation.

Core element 1: Rituals, signs, symbols

Each brand owns signs and symbols that are distinctive from others brands (as seen in section 1.3.2):

• The Logo
• The Monogram – formed by the creator's initials
• The Trademarks – that act as a quality guarantee
• Iconic Historic Signs

Core element 2: Behaviors, customs, attitudes, roles

Each brand expects all its employees to adopt and respect its customs, behaviors and specific roles:

- The respect for historic characters that wrote the brand's legend: the creator, the family.
- The way to inspire a certain "art of living": the world of gracious living, old world culture and refinement.
- The *"savoir faire"* in organizing and celebrating a luxury event: for instance the 100-year brand anniversary, a customer's welcome event ...
- The "brand's *touch*" to develop strong relationships with the luxury and business community.
- The very unique way of getting the creator in the "limelight" while the businessman remain behind the scenes.
- The art of communicating as a Brand Ambassador.

Thanks to these key behaviors, customs and specific roles, a brand and its people remain distinctive from all other brands.

Core element 3: Memories, stories, values, ideas, sense of belonging

Each brand has its founding story, its history and its values:

- Why are rituals so important? Because rituality is reassuring: the repetitive nature of things confers a form of harmony and stability. Rituals fix the individual in time: things done yesterday and today and which will be done again tomorrow. In a sense rituals create an emotional and physical link between the product/brand and the consumer. Think of the opening of a champagne bottle or discovering the dial of a Jaeger Le Coultre Reverso watch.
- All luxury brands have tales to tell: the history of their founder or legendary stories, like the Gucci family saga and the revival by Tom Ford, or enchanting stories about the brand's origins, such as Ferragamo "the Shoemaker of the Stars" or Cartier "The Jeweler of Kings, the King of Jewelers." These can even

be stories that are entirely made up, like that of Tod's which claimed that their loafers had been worn by John Kennedy or David Niven.

• Stories are also there to speak of the quality of the products: "Every Bvlgari creation is permeated with a spirit of excellence, hence the attention to detail and the research for absolute quality, typical of each product ... Every Bvlgari product is an object that undergoes meticulous examination in order to be coherent with Bvlgari's tradition in quality .... ." BottegaVeneta will say: "Every bag is completely handmade, there is no computer cutting involved at all. Every skin is inspected for any imperfections – a lot of leather is wasted because of this – but the result is a perfectly handmade bag."

This brand storytelling – which is essentially cultural – reinforces the internal consistency and the external bond with the customer and therefore the sense of belonging, both internal and external.

Core element 4: Ethics and vision of the world

Authentic luxury brands all share similar ethics:

• They fulfill customers' dreams and do what is necessary to satisfy all their desires and preferences.
• They preserve the brand's DNA mystery: the craftsmanship experience, the secret about historic "savoir faire," the creation process.
• They support the small companies that are critical to their creative dimension (embroiderers, watch makers, engravers, etc.) even in tough economic times.

Each of these core elements nurture and grow the content of the four distinct luxury corporate cultures that we have identified along two key criteria: their ability to mix their strong identity (Ego Centric) and their real openness to the outside environment (Eco Systemic) (see Figure 1.24).

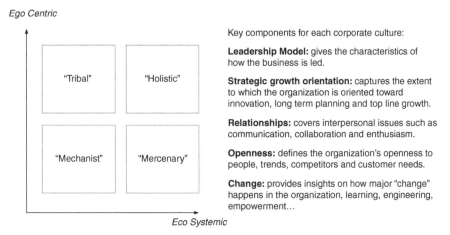

Figure 1.24   The four distinct luxury corporate cultures

Source: Adapted from J.C. Fauvet (2004): L'élan sociodynamique, Editions d'Organisation.

The two dominant Luxury Corporate Cultures, **"Tribal" versus "Mercenary"** show specific characteristics (see Figure 1.25):

1.5.1   "Tribal dominance" corporate culture

Leadership Model: A very entrepreneurial business model that is inspired by a charismatic leader or a family guide which sometimes is both the creator and the business developer.

Strategic-growth orientation: Marketing development is critical and distribution is selective and controlled (corporate-owned stores and selective wholesale).

Relationships: People who work in this corporate culture are very proud to do so; they usually start, grow and stay with the company having the mindset of an exclusive "social brand membership."

Openness: Because all the energy is focused on the inside, this model could remain ignorant of the competitors and be removed from both street trends and customers' expectations.

"Change": Innovation and change are inspired by the tribal leader or family guide.

Examples: Cartier, Hermès, Rolex, etc.

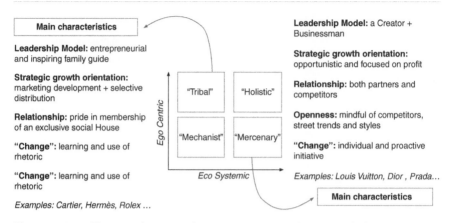

Figure 1.25 The two dominant luxury corporate cultures: "Tribal" versus "Mercenary"

1.5.2 "Mercenary dominance" corporate culture

Leadership Model: A leadership duo of a creator and a business-man where the Artistic Director is in the limelight while the manager runs the business remaining behind the scene.

Strategic-growth orientation: The consequence of the leadership duo inspires an opportunistic and profitable strategic growth focus where investments in design of new products must have commercial success.

Relationships: People who work in such a corporate culture are both business partners and competitors with taste for challenges and achieving success under pressure.

Openness: "Data crunching" what the competitors do and how they do it is a business obsession, with great attention given to street trends, the styles and customers' satisfaction.

"Change": Innovation, change and risk taking are the permanent guidelines of each person.

Examples: Louis Vuitton, Prada, etc.

The other two luxury corporate cultures **"Mechanist"** vs. **"Holistic"** demonstrate the following characteristics (see Figure 1.26):

1.5.3 "Mechanist dominance" corporate culture

Leadership Model: The Fast-Moving Consumer Goods industry model.

Leadership Model: "FMCG industry"

Strategic growth orientation: consumer goods

Relationships: stakeholders

Openness: sales oriented

"Change": unexpected and process

Examples: L'Oreal, Vertu, ...

Main characteristics

Ego Centric

"Tribal" | "Holistic"

"Mechanist" | "Mercenary"

Eco Systemic

Main characteristics

Leadership Model: Global, innovative

Strategic growth orientation: network of partnerships

Relationship: partners, experience sharing

Openness: partnership with consumer, suppliers and competitors

"Change": constant and proactive

Examples: luxury brands of the future

Figure 1.26   The other luxury corporate culture: "Mechanist" versus "Holistic"

Strategic-Growth Orientation: The importance of product development and communication are very high, with a strong focus on customer satisfaction.

Relationships: People are "stakeholders" dedicated to the brand.

Openness: Very high with a focus on "scorecard" sales achievements and key competitors' successes.

"Change": Is a permanent top-down process, all too often unexpected.

Examples: Vertu, L'Oréal, etc.

1.5.4   "Holistic" corporate culture (see Figure 1.26)

Leadership Model: A very open, holistic and innovative model, where initiative and cooperation with customers are key.

Strategic-Growth Orientation: The weight of creation is very high with customer participation for some products; controlled channel distribution including e-luxury; emphasis on superior service.

Relationships: *"The art of letting go"* and *"to break the rules"* enable people to both create, develop their network and bring added value to the end customer.

Openness: *Holistic* itself refers to an open system, with interdependence and interaction with both market, competitors and customers.

"Change": Innovation and change are permanent and a both proactive and collective initiative.

Examples: The luxury brands of the future.

1.6   The four key populations to manage

As with other industries, the luxury industry is evolving today in both a shifting global landscape and a tough economic climate that impacts people challenges: increasing demand for talented executives and designers faces a shrinking talent pool (see Figure 1.27).

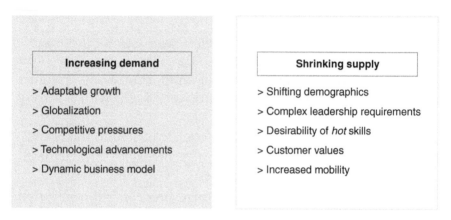

Increasing demand

> Adaptable growth

> Globalization

> Competitive pressures

> Technological advancements

> Dynamic business model

Shrinking supply

> Shifting demographics

> Complex leadership requirements

> Desirability of *hot* skills

> Customer values

> Increased mobility

Figure 1.27   Luxury industry people challenges

Companies are in search of **excellence** in terms of **quality**, **style** and **innovation** in order to better serve the needs of their clients. Their corporate reputation and brand image is thus strongly linked with **intangible assets**, sociological and psychological factors, while having to anticipate and manage economic factors such as cost, volume manufacturing, license fees, and the defining of distribution channels across markets. Competition is severe, with the development of global players, global brands and global distribution networks and companies have to balance the need for **global integration** with the need for **local responsiveness**.

Ultimately, companies are **competing for talent**: They need to attract and develop the best **designers**, **retailers**, **managers** and **experts** for their workshops and manufacture-specific jobs and general *savoir-faire*.

In such a context, those that lead luxury brands must handle two main issues (see Figure 1.28), which can be seen as a virtuous circle *if* done successfully:

1. *To preserve the key elements that have passed on from generation to generation to nurture the brand's DNA*
   To achieve this it is necessary to always keep in mind what **the founder/creator's vision and heritage are** and to use them very carefully. Likewise it is crucial to understand the core element you work with – **the craftsmanship experience** – which is unique and specific to each category (watches, jewelry, fashion, etc.). This effort must be made in order to build strong relationships with the people that are in charge of the historic and fundamental know-how that they have learnt from their peers and mentors. Last but not least, it is necessary to understand the critical elements of luxury brand management: **control of production** and **of distribution**.

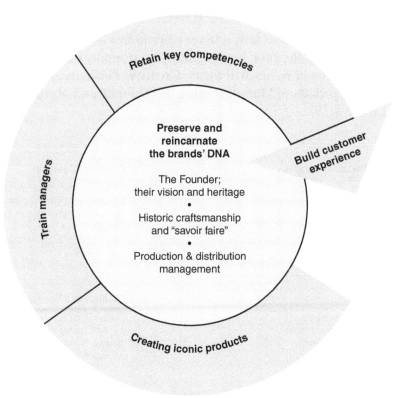

Figure 1.28 The luxury brand's purpose: the virtuous circle

2. *To build an attractive "place to work" that inspires passion and trust in those that have to nurture, to grow and to revitalise the Brand's DNA*

   A major issue facing luxury brands is to attract talents that are able **to create new products** expected by the customers; new products that must be both distinctive and in line with the previous iconic best sellers. Another critical point is **to train managers** continually on the specific corporate culture and luxury business "insights" that enable them to be more professional and to behave as brand ambassadors. Simultaneously, it is crucial **to retain key competencies**, particularly those who grew up with the brand including: people responsible for the key skills (stones expert, watchmaker, stylist, etc.) as well as exceptional sales staff that are critical "contact points" for customers. Finally, providing a broad range of services that builds a strong and personalized relationship with customers: Delivering the highest levels of service and telling stories about the brand that will keep customer loyalty alive.

This strong belief about how a luxury brand has to be managed has led us to identify the four key populations around which the major talent management issues will focus: Creative/ Designer, Executive/ Manager, Workshop/Manufacturing Workforce and Retail Staff (see Figure 1.29).

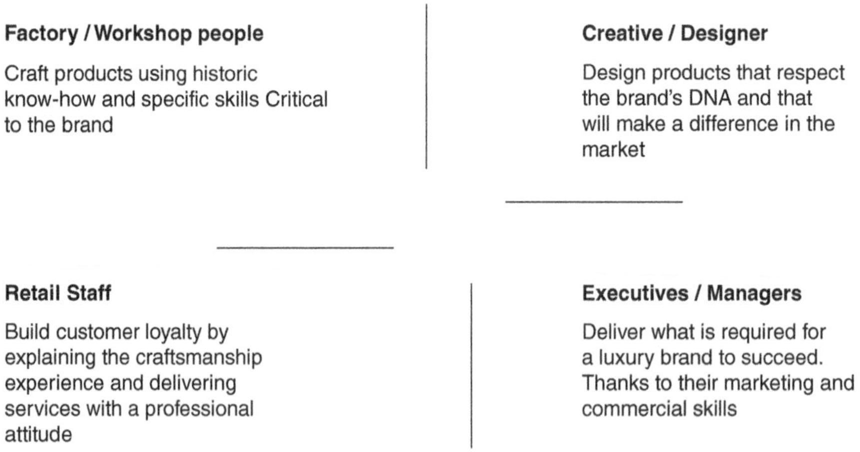

Factory / Workshop people

Craft products using historic know-how and specific skills Critical to the brand

Creative / Designer

Design products that respect the brand's DNA and that will make a difference in the market

Retail Staff

Build customer loyalty by explaining the craftsmanship experience and delivering services with a professional attitude

Executives / Managers

Deliver what is required for a luxury brand to succeed. Thanks to their marketing and commercial skills

Figure 1.29 The four key populations to manage

Creative/Designer

They design the products that respect the brand's DNA and make a difference in the market.

Executive/Managers

They deliver what it is required to ensure the brand's success thanks to their marketing, financial and commercial knowledge and skills.

Workshop/Manufacturing Workforce

They craft the products using historic know-how and specific skills critical to the brand.

Retail Staff

Their professional attitudes allow them to build customer loyalty by discovering customer needs and desires, explaining the craftsmanship experience and delivering critical services.

These four populations have specific capabilities and particular skills and professional behaviors that make them distinctive; a mix is not found in others industries.

In the following chapters, we will discuss examples and developments for each population segment, concerning recruitment, international career paths and perspectives as well as other key *talent* challenges such as compensation systems and coaching.

Likewise, we will examine in detail the specific management issues that concern each of them directly. By looking at such issues as how to manage family succession planning, how to recruit and lead specific roles, how to anticipate the luxury leaders' future challenges and prepare the leadership of the future, we will be able to provide concrete and tangible recommendations for each of these key populations.

The origin of the Kelly bag: Prince Rainier of Monaco and Grace Kelly holding an Hermès 'sac à dépêches' bag hiding her pregnancy (*Life* magazine cover 1956)

PART 2

Portraits and jobs in luxury

Introduction

There are two main objectives to Part 2:

To illustrate the four key populations working in the luxury industry:
1. executives
2. creator/designer
3. retail staff
4. workshop/ manufacturing workforce

To present critical profiles that define each population and provide useful advice for working with them

Each population will be examined through:

- Portraits, which focus on how real people have built and driven their career path thanks to their leadership style, personal temperament and cultural background.
- Representative job descriptions, which use relevant Human Resources criteria. Given the broad range of jobs that we could have chosen to look at, we decided to concentrate on those jobs that are good entry points when starting in the luxury industry. One should ideally have held such a role and mastered its associated skills and behavior before proceeding to a senior leadership role in a luxury brand.

These are as follows:

a. *Executive*: Country Manager, Marketing Development Director, Production Director
b. *Creative*: Collection Director, Senior Fashion Designer, Visual Merchandiser Manager
c. *Manufacturer/Workshop*: The watch manufacturing model; insights into a High Jewelry Workshop and an illustration of the craftsmanship experience behind the famous Kelly bag
d. *Retail*: Store Director, Sales Staff, Sales Expert

- Contextual observations and case studies designed to provide an in-depth understanding of how certain people from these populations work and how best to work with them.

2.1 Executive talent

- Three exemplary leaders of the luxury industry: Nicolas Hayek, Jean Louis Dumas and Alain Dominique Perrin
- Representative Job Descriptions
  - Country Manager
  - Marketing Development Manager
  - Director of Production
- Three key insights: executive talent in context
  - The Brand Manager Profile
  - How the International Commercial function works
  - The top 100 luxury board members profiles

2.1.1 Executive Portraits: three exemplary leaders of the luxury industry

Nicolas Hayek (1928–2010)

The "Industrialist" who saved the Swiss watch industry.

Engineer and dynamic entrepreneur, Nicolas Hayek, was born in Lebanon and became a Swiss citizen. He started his career as a consultant, focused largely on R&D and innovation to lead complex and international projects.

In the early 1980s, the Swiss watch industry faced looming catastrophe as it failed to realize the importance of quartz watches, even though the quartz watch had been invented in Switzerland in 1967. The Japanese were undercutting Swiss manufacturers with a glut of inexpensive but accurate and reliable watches, reducing Switzerland's global market share to 20 percent. Industry analysts argued that with its high labor costs, Switzerland could never compete. With the country's two largest watch manufacturers close to financial collapse, the Swiss bank UBS turned to Nicolas Hayek as a consultant.

He quickly realized that no one doubted the quality of Swiss watches but that the Swiss industrial landscape ignored the changing global environment. He concluded that the manufacturing process had become detached from a clear understanding of the market. In addition, he decided that the customer had to be sold on the idea of wearing a watch as a personal statement.

As a result, in 1986, he was appointed to manage the newly formed consolidated company that was to become the Swatch Group. It would control 18 leading brands including Blancpain, Breguet, Longines, Omega and Rado.

Jean Louis Dumas (1938–2010)

The "Creator" who grew the house of Hermès from a leather goods business into a major league luxury brand.

Jean Louis Dumas was the great, great grandson of Thierry Hermès, who founded the famous label in 1837 as a harness maker. Famously elegant, and noted for his inventive and curious mind, Dumas is widely regarded as the driving force in Hermes' remarkable blossoming over the past three decades.

He assumed the leadership of Hermès in 1978 and with a free, sometimes audacious hand, Mr Dumas began shaking things up: He hired exciting new designers (including Tomas Maier and

Martin Margiela), extended the company's lines, expanded internationally and invested in companies like the glassware maker Saint Louis, the tableware company Puiforcat, the fashion House of Jean Paul Gaultier, the German camera company Leica and the London shoemaker John Lobb.

An intrepid voyageur with a fascination for remote civilizations and distant cultures, Dumas used his experiences to enrich Hermès creativity: Under his management, for example, he famously recreated Kelly bags in raw rubber supplied by a primitive Amazonian tribe.

Mr Dumas, who retired in 2006 because of ill health, always carried an old Leica with him, taking pictures constantly and always sketching in a small notepad: his office at the Pantin Ateliers was that of a Creative Director and hardly one of a CEO!

Alain Dominique Perrin (1942)

The "Marketer" who defined the idea of "modern luxury."[1]

Alain Dominique Perrin – "ADP" to the people he works with – was born in Nantes (France) in 1942. Having been a distinguished antique dealer, he joined the Cartier Lighter Company in 1969 as commercial attaché, before becoming Managing Director the following year.

In 1976 he was named President of "Must de Cartier" and rose to become the head of Cartier International and Cartier SA. He was responsible for the renaissance and international development of Cartier, and having fashioned a whole range of "Must de Cartier" items, he also distinguished himself in his battle against counterfeiting, of which he was a pioneer.

As an active entrepreneur, ADP founded several critical institutions dedicated to education and the promotion of culture:

• The Cartier Foundation for Contemporary Art in Paris, which pays tribute to contemporary art while promoting the name of Cartier in the world of culture (1984).

- The International Salon for High Jewellery (SIHH), followed a year later by the Training Institute for High Jewellery (IFHH), whose objectives are to preserve watch-making traditions (1991).
- He also created the Institut Superieur de Marketing du Luxe (ISML).

At the beginning of 1999 he took over the leadership of the Richemont Group, the second largest group in the world of luxury, specializing in jewelry, watch–making and accessories across international brands including Cartier, Van Cleef & Arpels, Jaeger le Coultre, IWC, Montblanc and Dunhill. Since 2003, he has been an Executive Director of Compagnie Financière Richemont.

2.1.2   Why did they lead this industry? Lessons to be learned

Lesson 1: All three have **strong cultural backgrounds, acquired through their families and their education,** which provided them with international exposure to cultural and business diversities. These early experiences provided them with a strong sense of self, highly sociable personalities and very positive mindsets which made them comfortable with the people who "play and spend" in the luxury environment.

Lesson 2: All of them have demonstrated great sensitivity to *family business heritage* and real passion for the craftsmanship factor:
- Respecting the quality of the Swiss watch industry and particularly the golden age of watchmaking (N. Hayek).
- Pursuing and expanding of the vision of Thierry Hermès (J. L. Dumas).
- Reincarnating and developing the brand's DNA, as inherited from founder and historic creator Louis Cartier (ADP).

Lesson 3: Their leadership sense, which would score highly in terms of emotional intelligence (EQ), cultural intelligence (CQ) and social intelligence (SQ), demonstrates their capacity to inspire passion and trust among all the people they met and/or worked with, all over the world.

Lesson 4: Each of them, as businessmen, **have initiated new ways to address the luxury business**, that are now acknowledged as standard in the industry.

- Nicolas Hayek changed the mindset of the Swiss watch industry by providing a new business model to watch manufacturers.
- Jean Louis Dumas – as both CEO and Creative Director of Hermès[2] – welcomed a broad range of new designers that boosted the international development of his brand.
- ADP innovated the marketing and communication of a luxury brand with a major initiative: the creation of an accessible entry line – the " Must de Cartier" collection.

2.1.3   Three executive job descriptions

Among the many Executive/Managerial positions that exist, we will examine three relevant job descriptions in detail in order to shed some light on this diverse population: Country Manager, Marketing Development Manager and Director of Production.

- These roles allow us to understand the essence of a luxury brand. Acting as a brand ambassador in a local market, launching a new range of products or managing the diverse people in a manufacturing/workshop environment are all critical distinctions of luxury industry.
- Each of these Executive jobs is key due to their direct accountability to the company's global P&L. In other words, each of them generates contributive economic value for the brand.
- Achieving an exceptional record in any of these three roles could provide direct access to a better career position and even a chance to become a board member. For example, a successful Country Manager could step up to become a Regional or International Commercial Director or a Production Director may evolve to become an Operations Director.

The Country Manager

The Country Manager is the person who acts as the "CEO of the company" but only for one specific market. Their challenge is to develop the brand's growth and awareness in line with the strategy and procedures of the parent company using local staff. Understanding the cultural differences of employees and customers is key to succeeding in this role (see Figure 2.1).

Country Manager

Role	• **Lead the country's business development** Responsible for all P&L accountability Ensure the brand integrity and notoriety and improve the financial results Establish country's 3 year plans • **Manage operations according to company strategy and procedures** Drive sales growth to build the global brand image which successfully captures and develops local and international clientele Provide on going analysis of the local competition, positioning of the brand and the quality of the presence Build up a soild and profitable distribution base • **Manage all teams, ensuring the development of competence and performance to exceed customers expectations of service**
Skills	• **Capacity to guide the development of all retail/wholesales activities** • **Ability to develop a corporate culture that exemplifies the values and quality of the brand** • **Leadership to effectively oversee all functions of the business ensuring productivity of all resources and employees**
Behavior	• **Insprirational leader with strong personal flair and the ability to stay connected with key people in the brand's HQ organization** • **Strong social skills to build solid relationships within the luxury/fashion and business community** • **Talent and good communication skills to act as a brand ambassador**
Experience required	• **University degree, MBA** • **Ten to fifteen years professional experience with operations backround in Marketing/Commercial in the luxury industry**

Figure 2.1 Country Manager job description

The Marketing Development Manager

This individual is responsible for developing new products that will continuously keep the luxury customer engaged by the brand. This job combines the product launching process and of market/business intelligence skills. Their aim is to launch appealing and enticing new products that revitalize the brand's heritage and founder's vision (see Figure 2.2).

Marketing Development Manager

Role

- **Manage the development process of a product range**

  Deliver a product brief to the Studio upon market detailed analysis, the competition and consumer needs

  Define the collection plan and coordinate the Studio, Developers, Sourcing during the prototype production process

  Target the ideal range, constantly looking to increase margin while ensuring brand integrity

- **Define and coordinate the product launch**

  Develop launch plan along with Logistics, Production and the Regions (timing by zone, assortments level by stores, etc)

  Oversee the development of the operational launch tools: product books, packaging, VM, internet, training tools, etc. to support sales

  Present products to Retail/Wholesale during Showrooms/Sales sessions

- **Deliver market and business intelligence**

  Provide relevant follow through and ongoing statistical information on sales performance and market trends

  Participate in the Marketing budget and 3 years plan redaction

---

Skills

- **Excellent communication and promotional skills and talent to persuade and coordinate others in a multicultural environment**
- **Ability to quickly grasp the key business drivers in the luxury industry: market trends and customer expectations**
- **Strong negotiation skills**

Behavior

- **Both creative and conceptual**
- **A keen sense for organization and priorities with a focus on "figures" and cost**
- **Good understanding of the marketing role in the operations value chain (CRM, merchandising, supply chain)**

Experience required

- **University Degree or MBA and 3 years professional experience in marketing**
- **Fluency in English. Italian a plus in the fashion & leather goods industry**

Figure 2.2   Marketing Development Manager job description

The Director of Production

The Director of Production is the *industrial* expert of the luxury brand, responsible for manufacturing products and delivering them to distributors on time. The job involves dealing with complex technical issues with the support of diverse team incorporating many different skills and specialized 'savoir-faire' (see Figure 2.3).

Director of Production

Role	• **Drive industrial production development policy in line with brand strategy**
	Responsible for the 3 year industrial strategic policy and forecast, accordingly to production development outcomes
	Responsible for the quality of craftsmanship and application of the brand's savoir faire at all production and development stages
	• **Manage the operating and change processes**
	Implement the tools necessary to support production of crafted products
	Provide on-going analysis against best practices in the industry
	• **Lead and manage several teams of highly skilled professionals**
	Coach these professionals in their working practices
	Deliver structured methodology that addresses workshop/manufacturing problems
Skills	• **Thorough knowledge of the main production and management techniques**
	• **Capacity to work hand-in-hand with a wide range of professionals and generations of experts, designers/stylists, engineers , ...**
	• **Ability to lead production/development of crafted products including after-sales experience**
Behavior	• **Positive and entrepreneurial temperament that can inspire workshop/ manufacturing members**
	• **Astute and "hands on" engineering focus to solve complex or technical issues**
Experience required	• **Degree in Engineering, MBA**
	• **Minimum ten years professional experience in a similar environment**
	• **Fluency in English; a good command of Italian or French a plus**

Figure 2.3   Director of Production job description

2.1.4   Three key insights: executive talent in context

The following **insight** will provide further insights into the responsibilities and behavior of luxury Executives.

- **Insight 1** looks at the large spectrum of knowledge, management skills and personal attributes required to lead a luxury brand.
- **Insight 2** illustrates how a luxury brand may address its dual-channel challenges.
- **Insight 3** presents the key characteristics of the luxury's top 100 board members and raises critical questions facing the industry today.

Insight 1: The Luxury Brand Manager profile

"There is no business like luxury where the brand manager's role is so emotional and nearly an art, it tries to blend the magic and the apparent irrationality of the creative process with the logic and reasoning of marketing and business' requirement." Carlo Valerio, CEO Istituto Europeo di Design, Milan (former CEO Emmanuel Ungaro)

A Luxury Brand Manager is a mix of three different things (see Figure 2.4):

Figure 2.4   The Luxury Brand Manager profile

1. **Personal Leadership Style:** a Brand Manager is overall a *worldwide brand ambassador* with strong social skills to build relationships within the luxury/fashion and business communities and the savoir-faire to present the brand's vision to the

→

customers, telling them the stories that engender the pleasure of buying. S(h)e has also talent and humility *to work closely with creatives/designers* and to stay behind the scenes, when necessary

> *"our job at Van Cleef & Arpels is to reincarnate what happened in 1896: the wedding of Estelle Arpels and Alfred Van Cleef... and to tell stories about more than a hundred years of emotions – 5 weeks in balloon – a journey in Paris –... to transform our today's client dream into VCA unique piece"*
>
> Excerpts from **Stanislas De Quercize**, CEO & President of Van Cleef & Arpels, the IHT luxury Heritage conference in London, 9 November 2010

2. **Competencies:** the Brand Manager, thanks to his/her international experience and personal background, has a *point of view on what luxury is about.* She/he also knows how to *inspire passion and trust* to all the people (s)he works with, creating for them the organizational space and resources where they can be truly committed.

3. **Cultural background:** the luxury environment requires an *obsession with perfection* regarding products, services and professional behavior. Therefore her/his education and sensitivity enable her/him to cope with the family business "codes" (when necessary), respecting the **brand's heritage** while leading **business development.**

> *"the company's signature trench coat, the icon product created by Thomas Burberry – the House founder – makes our past and present and its reincarnation stays relevant in the digital world"*
>
> Excerpts from **Angela Ahrendt** CEO and **Christopher Bailey** Chief Creative Officer of Burberry – the IHT luxury Heritage conference in London, 9 November 2010

We believe that the Brand Manager is more of a Leader than a Manager; something that will be explored in later chapters (see Part 4 – Leading and Managing Talent).

Insight 2: Restructuring organizations – an executive challenge

The following is a real case study which looks at how a Chief Executive must create a new Executive role and an organizational restructure in order to meet the demands of a company with different distribution channels.

The company:
A luxury brand that operates in different categories (watches, jewelry and leather accessories products) and manages both retail and wholesale networks. They have their own exclusive stores, but also sell products (in one case watches and a select number of fine jewelry pieces; in the other, leather accessories) to exclusive distributors. A new CEO is appointed to develop the brand's awareness and the global profitability. The Brand has no Creative Director.

The business challenges:
- Grow the value of the business while retaining "best in class" status;
- Find, within the company, a leader with strong commercial and management skills who would be able to design an appropriate International Commercial division that ensures coherence between the two channels in order to:
  - Balance retail and wholesale networks in cities where the two systems co-exist;
  - Homogenize the brand's DNA in the two systems;
  - Develop HR mobility between the two networks.

The new International Commercial Director will be required to:
- Build an International Commercial team of diverse talent and management skills developed within the company.
- Design a new international commercial organization with four major departments: commercial strategy/store concept and visual merchandising/stores staff/clients. (see Figure 2.5).

$\rightarrow$

- Assign specific department objectives to the four Department Managers:

Figure 2.5 Organization chart of the new International Commercial Department

The Commercial Strategy Department: company network scaling, audit and coordination for EMEA, Americas and Asia regions and pricing & margin control. Its global objective is to ensure the commercial balance between retail and wholesale systems.

The Stores Concept & Visual Merchandising Department: Its main objective is to deliver visual consistency globally.

The Stores Staff Department: HR management tools and approaches: reward, mobility, internal communications, managing challenges and training. Its particular objective is to enhance the commercial skills by using appropriate talent.

The Clients Department: client database, call center, website, direct marketing in coordination with other company support functions (IT, supply chain, merchandising, stock). The key objective is to provide a wide range of services to the POS and the final client.

Insight 3: The top 100 luxury board members in profile

Here are some sobering facts about the state of luxury brand leadership, gleaned from profiling those who serve on the boards of firms in this sector, including CEOs, Artistic Directors, Sales Directors and Finance Directors. Critical findings are as follows[3]:

1. **65 percent of luxury board members have spent the majority of their careers in the luxury industry** or related sectors (e. g. fashion, retail, luxury goods). Of the rest, more than 10 percent came from FMCGs.
2. **75 percent of luxury board members are Europeans,** of which 35 percent are French, 20 percent Italian, 10 percent Swiss, 5 percent German, 5 percent British, and 15 percent are American.
3. **10 percent of luxury board members are the son or daughter of the family company founder**.
4. **20 percent of luxury board members are female** – 10 percent are CEO; the majority of the rest are responsible for Artistic or Marketing areas.
5. **Less than 15 percent of the Top 100 luxury board members have a MBA degree.**
6. **52 is the average age for luxury board members.**
7. **The lack of Asian nationals among the Top 100 luxury board members and in senior leadership positions is a critical issue.**

What does that tell us?
The two first points indicate that Europeans, who have built a career in this industry, find it a very attractive and comfortable place to stay. **This begs the question: Could their view of global business be myopic?**

Belonging to the original creator's family remains the easiest way to lead a luxury brand. **However, do they have the qualifications to deal with new global realities?**

$\rightarrow$

The representation of females in key leadership positions gets a high score in the luxury industry compared to other industries (20 percent vs. 4.5 percent). **But, is that a sufficient representation for a market in which women easily represent the growing base of customers?**

In the shifting landscape of a globalized world, investing in business education programs is a top priority for a lot of industries, except for luxury industry. **So, will competitor brands with more business savvy overtake them?**

Succession planning for the current leading managers is a critical issue that a lot of brands must face urgently. **However, who will replace them as they retire?**

To this date, just a few Asian people have leadership responsibilities in the Top 100, raising the **question; how can companies that hope to operate in countries such as China and India grasp the importance of understanding their different cultures?**

The critical questions raised by the profiles of luxury's Top 100 board members will be explored in subsequent chapters.

2.2 Creative/design talent

- A creative/designer portrait Frank Nuovo, the vision of luxury in a handset
- Three creative/designer Job Descriptions
  - Collection Director
  - Senior Designer
  - Visual Merchandiser
- Four key insights: creative/designers in context
  - The creative luxury profile: "keeper of the brand"
  - Organization chart of design function at Bally
  - The ladies' shoes collection calendar at Bally
  - The Hermès/Eurocopter helicopter

2.2.1 A creative portrait: Frank Nuovo[4]

The visionary behind luxury in a handset

When you ask Frank Nuovo about how he first got the idea to create a precious handcrafted cell phone and he starts to talk geography, you may well think that he's not going to answer you, until you realize that the story of Vertu is also the story of Nuovo himself, the various places to which he feels an attachment, and his deep curiosity for foreign places, cultures and influences.

Nuovo tells you about California, where he got his creative sense by growing up in the artistically diverse community of Monterey and earned his degree from the Art Center College of Design in Pasadena, renowned for its programs in product, automotive, communications and industrial design. This is where he got the personal conviction that innovation must combine technology, usability and style with user-centric design. This vision successfully took shape at BMW Designworks where, as Design Director for nine years, he conceived consumer electronics, medical instruments, automotive products, furnishings, architectural interiors and car interiors. He then joined Nokia in 1995 where he was Head of Design for 11 years. His touch brought Nokia a lot of success: By forming a team of designers made up of 30 nationalities he was able to open the company up to the world. He demonstrated tremendous mental agility, not only leading design strategy but also following-up projects right through marketing and communication, being, for example, very active in brand development and renewal. The incredible result of his vision and attitude: Nokia's position as the world's sixth most valuable brand (Interbrand, 2006).

Nuovo also refers to his family roots in Sicily, and how it gave him the taste to look for beauty in everything and the conviction that even daily functional objects can be beautiful. This was the premise behind the creation of Vertu in 1997: to bring luxury and design into a product category that, until then, was seen exclusively as mass-market. Vertu now proudly stands shoulder to shoulder with other luxury brands and Nuovo has essentially invented a new product category in a very traditional industry. This is Nuovo's strength: Think out of the box, mix different influences, combine tradition, hand-crafting and technology, or, as luxury people would say, heritage and modernity: The essence of true luxury.

2.2.2 Three creative/designer job descriptions

The following job descriptions are particularly representative of this dynamic population within the luxury industry: Collection Director, Senior Designer and Visual Merchandiser.

- All of these creative jobs demand exceptional skills and personal characteristics (creative eye, true flair, a strong healthy ego, etc.) that must work in tandem with the Creative Director's personality; acting as his/her right-hand, providing stylistic or creative input, dealing with important decisions – all while staying in the shadows when the spotlight is on.
- Each job combines complex and sophisticated techniques, savoir-faire, manufacturing processes and aesthetic and stylistic research and a sharp eye for trends. In the brand's studio or atelier these particular skills may be very specific and very unique. They will be passed on from master to mentee during a demanding apprenticeship.
- Management skills are also critical in these creative jobs in order to:
  - Inspire diverse teams of multicultural talent, skills and strong personalities;
  - Keep the team from cracking under the pressure, focused to deliver on time and with careful attention to quality and aesthetics.

The Collection Director

He or she is the Creative Director's right–hand, assuming the operational development of the collection right though to its presentation to buyers while inspiring a positive spirit within the studio and team. Thanks to a combination of pragmatism and creativity, the Collection Director will ensure that collections are delivered on time (see Figure 2.6).

	Collection Director
Role	• **In close collaboration with the Artistic Director, define the stylistic direction for the new collections while respecting the brand's aesthetic heritage and business objectives**
	Transcribe the brief of the Artistic Director to the designers; act as a guide for the designers throughout the creation process
	Define the collection plan along with the designers and marketing Communicate frequently with other Collection Directors to ensure a coherence of all the collections in the range
	• **Monitor the development of the collections, until their presentation to buyers**
	Oversee delivery schedule of prototypes and validate prototypes
	Control product merchandising for showrooms and sales sessions. In the fashion industry, work on fashion shows.
	• **Act as a "brand keeper"**
	Define the "image" products and, with PR and Communication, define the tools to support them, while keeping a balanced message with "commercial" products
Skills	• **Capacity to be a pragmatic brand visionary, always balancing brand heritage, market trends and the company's business targets**
	• **Ability to inspire trust to both executives managers and the studio/product creation committee**
	• **Creativity and taste associated with a good knowledge of production processes**
Behavior	• **Positive spirit, able to forge working teams with strong multi-cultural personalities**
	• **Obsessed with perfection, quality and attentive to details**
	• **Able to maintain energy and focus and to work under pressure in the fashion and leather goods industries**
Experience required	• **Higher Education-International Design School**
	• **A minimum of ten years professional experience with an excellent knowledge of product development**
	• **Fluency in English; a good command of French or Italian a definite advantage**

Figure 2.6   Collection Director job description

The Senior Designer

This job mixes "savoir-faire" (know-how), production processes and stylistic research. Strong social skills and diplomacy are often required to handle the Artistic Director's personality and to work well in this very emotional and pressured environment (see Figure 2.7).

	Senior Designer
Role	• **Create new products in line with the Artistic Director's brief and requirements expressed in the collection plan** Realize 2D drawings integrating the main technical details; when necessary, realize 3D mock-ups Ensure qualitative product development (mock-ups, prototypes, test collection, final fittings) working with developers and the workshops • **Provide accurate stylistic intelligence to the Artistic Director and the Collection Director** Attend professional fairs to research new materials and techniques in order to enrich the scope and appeal of the collections Follow-up the evolution of the key competitors' offering • **Ensure proper merchandising of product for showrooms and sales meetings**
Skills	• **Strong expertise in the techniques, savoir-faire and manufacturing/production processes** • **Comfortable with stylistic research** • **Capable of understanding the core market offering with a true flair for forecasting trends**
Behavior	• **Obsessed with perfection, quality and an eye for detail** • **Organized, rigorous and meticulous to provide effective support to the Collection Director** • **Persuasive of others with strong and multi-cultural personalities** • **Strong ability to work under pressure in the fashion and leather goods industries**
Experience required	• **Graduate from a Fashion/Creative School** • **Minimum of 5 years experience of which 2 or 3 in a similar position** • **Fluency in English; a good command of French or Italian a definite advantage**

Figure 2.7   Senior Designer job description

The Visual Merchandiser

His or her creative eye and merchandising expertise will have a strong visual impact on how the brand is perceived while supporting the sell-thru of products in store. This is a very hands-on operational role and he or she will be highly aware of emerging and innovative trends (see Figure 2.8).

	Visual Merchandiser
Role	• **Implement the VM strategy defined by HQ respecting the key criteria of aesthetics, commerciality and innovation**
	Define VM solutions that will generate strong impact and support sell-thru, working in close collaboration with marketing and design
	Brief external image agencies, being always driven to maintain a good price/quality ratio
	Follow-up mock-ups and validate prototypes
	• **Provide implementation assistance and training to in-store VM support staff**
	Create VM guidance books. Coordinate local contributors to ensure timely and proper product display
	Propose custom design solutions for wholesale POS, working closely with trade marketing, when necessary
	Ensure visual integrity of special events (store openings, CRM events, catwalks…)
	• **Provide accurate intelligence on VM evolution worldwide (materials, techniques, styles)**
Skills	• **Ability to partner with both creative and executive managers**
	• **Strong analytical/organizational sense to monitor facility and equipment logistics issues**
	• **Capacity to be the "keeper of the brand" when briefing external image agencies**
Behavior	• **A good luxury acumen to anticipate emerging and innovative trends**
	• **Very organized, rigorous and meticulous with a good creative eye**
	• **Hands-on operational with ability to work with diverse teams**
Experience required	• **Graduate from a Fashion/Creative School a plus**
	• **A minimum of 5 years experience of which 2 or 3 in a similar position**
	• **Fluency in English; a good command of French or Italian a definite advantage**

Figure 2.8 Visual Merchandiser job description

2.2.3 Four key insights: creative/design talent in context

The following will provide further details about the creative/designer profile, and related organizational and operational challenges:

- **Insight 1** looks at the complex mix of knowledge, creative skills and personal attributes that characterize creative/designer for a leading luxury brand.
- **Insight 2** illustrates how the design function was organized at Bally.

- **Insight 3** presents the complexity of the complete process of the ladies' shoes collection calendar at Bally.
- **Insight 4** illustrates the role of a designer when working with engineers on a project – the Hermès/Eurocopter helicopter.

Insight 1: The luxury creative profile: "keeper of the brand"

The ideal luxury creative profile is a mix of three different things (see Figure 2.9):

Personal leadership styles: Creatives travel extensively visiting fairs, exhibitions, competitor's stores; they see enormous amounts of products, they read magazines and from this gather encyclopedic references of products that provide them with a *global brand vision* and allow them to *interpret/distort the brand's aesthetics heritage.*

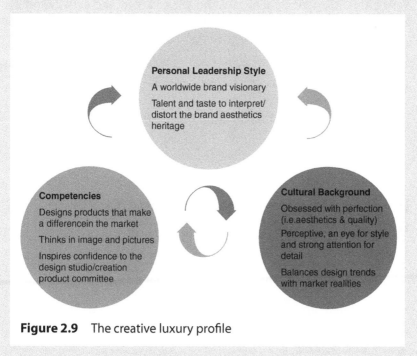

Figure 2.9   The creative luxury profile

→

"my job is not to destroy the past but to understand the essence of the House and to rebuild the dream for the women of today... being relevant"
> Quote from **Albert Elbaz**, the Creative Director of Lanvin – the IHT luxury Heritage conference in London, 9 November 2010.

Competencies: creative people are those who know what design will sell *and make a difference in the market.* Their designs are based on memory, on recent experiences and current concerns; their imagination is strictly visual: they *think in images and pictures*; and they have *to inspire confidence in the design studio*

Cultural background: the luxury environment demands from them a great *obsession for perfection* regarding products and services. They have therefore developed a perceptive sense with a *flair for style and strong attention to detail* and a pragmatic *business sense* to make their designs a commercial success.

The mixture of a **Vision**, **Creative Instinct** and **Business Sense** is very rare: Most designers lack business sense and will favor a much more top-down approach *"This is good for the brand because I have designed it"* which is the Aristocratic attitude that most French Couturiers and some British designers exemplify.

In the 21st century, luxury brands are about creation, business and overall customer satisfaction. It is the customer that will ultimately decide which brands meet their desires, their needs and their expectations.

Insight 2: Organization chart of the design function at Bally

The chart below highlights the way the design department was organized at Bally in 2001. We can note the following:

- The design and development functions were merged into a single unit to ensure the maximum fusion between 2D designs and prototyping.

$\rightarrow$

- **"Editors at Large"** – opinion leaders in the luxury world – were appointed in Paris, Hong Kong and New York to keep the company up to date on fashion trends and what the competition was doing while providing feedback on past and current collections.

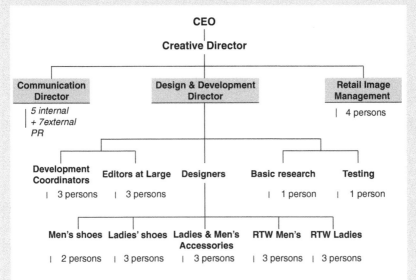

Figure 2.10   The organization chart of the design function at Bally

Source: Michel Chevalier and Gérald Mazzalovo (2008): Luxury Brand Management, a world of privilege, Wiley.

A total of 31 internal creative staff, plus other outside staff such as the Public Relations agency and the Editors-at-Large, were involved in the process (see Figure 2.10).

Insight 3: The ladies' shoes collection calendar at Bally

Figure 2.11[5] is a real example of calendar for a ladies' shoes collection, showing all the different steps and people involved, and the complexity of the complete process:

→

A Ladies' shoes collection is more likely be organized as lines, classified by construction, occasion for use, specific sole or materials. Each line will specify the desired retail price in its target market, as well as heel height and all the different materials that it can be made in.

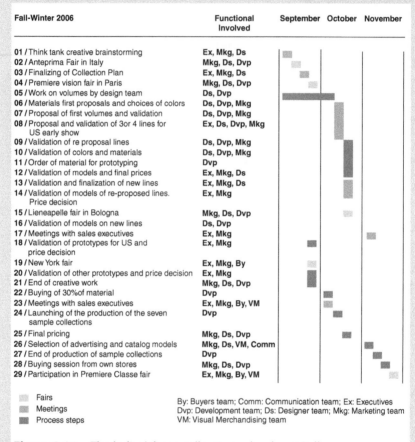

Fall-Winter 2006	Functional Involved	September	October	November
01 / Think tank creative brainstorming	Ex, Mkg, Ds			
02 / Anteprima Fair in Italy	Mkg, Ds, Dvp			
03 / Finalizing of Collection Plan	Ex, Mkg, Ds			
04 / Premiere vision fair in Paris	Mkg, Ds, Dvp			
05 / Work on volumes by design team	Ds, Dvp			
06 / Materials first proposals and choices of colors	Ds, Dvp, Mkg			
07 / Proposal of first volumes and validation	Ds, Dvp, Mkg			
08 / Proposal and validation of 3or 4 lines for US early show	Ex, Ds, Dvp, Mkg			
09 / Validation of re proposal lines	Ds, Dvp, Mkg			
10 / Validation of colors and materials	Ds, Dvp, Mkg			
11 / Order of material for prototyping	Dvp			
12 / Validation of models and final prices	Ex, Mkg, Ds			
13 / Validation and finalization of new lines	Ex, Mkg, Ds			
14 / Validation of models of re-proposed lines. Price decision	Ex, Mkg			
15 / Lieneapelle fair in Bologna	Mkg, Ds, Dvp			
16 / Validation of models on new lines	Ds, Dvp			
17 / Meetings with sales executives	Ex, Mkg			
18 / Validation of prototypes for US and price decision	Ex, Mkg			
19 / New York fair	Ex, Mkg, By			
20 / Validation of other prototypes and price decision	Ex, Mkg			
21 / End of creative work	Mkg, Ds, Dvp			
22 / Buying of 30%of material	Dvp			
23 / Meetings with sales executives	Ex, Mkg, By, VM			
24 / Launching of the production of the seven sample collections	Dvp			
25 / Final pricing	Mkg, Ds, Dvp			
26 / Selection of advertising and catalog models	Mkg, Ds, VM, Comm			
27 / End of production of sample collections	Dvp			
28 / Buying session from own stores	Mkg, Ds, Dvp			
29 / Participation in Premiere Classe fair	Ex, Mkg, By, VM			

　Fairs
　Meetings
　Process steps

By: Buyers team; Comm: Communication team; Ex: Executives
Dvp: Development team; Ds: Designer team; Mkg: Marketing team
VM: Visual Merchandising team

Figure 2.11　The ladies' shoes collection calendar at Bally

The **collection calendar** formalizes the important events in the collection's development process as agreed to by all the departments involved:

- Ordering materials for samples and production;
- Intermediary meetings to review the design progress;

- Final editing of the collection;
- Ordering for stores and so on.

It is the most referred to common tool of all the departments involved in collection development.

The number of professional fairs attended by the designers and merchandisers is also indicated, as well as the regular involvement of the commercial department right up until the presentation of the sample collection to wholesale clients and store buyers.

Insight 4: The Hermès/Eurocopter helicopter

In 2007 Hermès and Eurocopter unveiled the latest version of the aerospace group's VIP helicopter, the result of a major project bringing together persons with very different backgrounds and experiences: Hermès designers and Eurocopter engineers.

In this document[6] Gabriele Pezzini, Hermès Design Director and Corinne Poux-Bernard, Hermès Innovation Director present and discuss the issues and intricacies of working together on a common project.

In search of the "perfect" object

Gabriele Pezzini: Design, a term used at every turn, is often reduced to a decorative concept. However, designing does not mean just drawing a beautiful object. It means understanding, from a perspective that is fresh, an object in all its dimensions (function, aesthetics, structure) and taking into account the whole process of its creation (design, production, transportation, packaging, catalogue). A chair, for example, is an object whose design is emblematic: its shape, structure and functionality are indissociable. The history of design is also interspersed with designs of chairs. When I came to Hermès, I found it had that kind of an

→

approach – the combination of a desire for a "perfect" object with a respect for the creator and the craftsman. Could this approach apply to a helicopter? That is the challenge that Pierre-Alexis Dumas, Artistic Director of Hermès offered me. He knew my work (which he had seen expressed in things as simple as a candle holder) and knew that I was inclined to look at things with a critical eye. Needless to say, his offer caused me a few sleepless nights...

Corinne Poux-Bernard: Before Eurocopter and Hermès reached an agreement, we had to understand what each one expected from the project and from its partner. Hermès saw, in the helicopter, a field for the expression of its culture, based on function, harmony and balance. Eurocopter for its part, wished to secure a place in the VIP universe and achieve premium market legitimacy by partnering with a player from the world of luxury. It was already producing models for a high-class clientele, where the decors and marketing were entrusted to an outside company.

Gabriele Pezzini: We had to persuade Eurocopter to accept a precondition: our work is designing. There was no question of making the helicopter "prettier" or, as one might imagine in our case, just dressing up the interior in orange leather and fixing a logo on it – Hermès' distinguishing traits. We asked for carte blanche to work on the aircraft in its totality, to offer a different concept. We had to understand what a helicopter is: what its technical principles were, what happens in a flight, the behaviour of its users. We soon realized that the helicopter is a magnificent machine, but it had not been conceived with those who travelled in it in mind.

When engineers join hands with craftsmen

Corinne Poux-Bernard: The encounter between Hermès and Eurocopter is an encounter between a business of traditional craft where the decision lies in the hands of the Artistic Director and a large industrial group where decisions are taken by a group of individuals. To make dialogue possible, we called upon a third person – Gabriele Pezzini, who conveys the spirit of Hermès and who also has a thorough understanding of the industrial world.

→

We had very little time to complete the project, because the objective was to present the first model at the show in Atlanta. In fact, the helicopter saw the light of day within nine months. This performance was made possible by functioning in a project mode that was extremely reactive, independent of the hierarchical formalities that existed, and into which everyone threw themselves, body and soul, with a certain sense of excitement. The decision-makers at Eurocopter were really a driving force and did all they could to make a success of the project.

Designer and engineers: with a common goal

Gabriele Pezzini: What was actually the most complicated in the project was the encounter between the two worlds – craftsmanship and industry, or indeed three worlds, Eurocopter France and Eurocopter Germany – entities that do not have the same awareness of innovation. It took time to understand us. Yet, we found a point in common that was unexpected: the handcrafted nature of our work. Surprising as it may seem, we found that a helicopter was partly a handcrafted product. For example, the helicopter blades are manufactured by hand, and errors in their design can only be detected by the human eye. During our first visit to Eurocopter in Germany, we met with engineers who were very open-minded – this also shook up some of our preconceived ideas. Insofar as it was a question of producing an item that was functional and perfect, our visions converged, even though, as a designer, I expressed it in terms that seemed strange to engineers. An engineer confessed to me that the landing gear that Hermès designed was one he had dreamt about for a long time. Yet, what authority did I have to propose a new landing gear? Since this item is composed of aluminium tubes, my reflexes were identical to those that a chair would have evoked. In his book, 'Spoken into the Void' the architect, Adolf Loos, says that an engineer first works from intuition, and then verifies it by calculations. If he is a good engineer, his intuition bears out. At Eurocopter, I had the intuition and the engineers did the calculations. In fact, I have used this operating method while working on many other products. Working through design enabled Eurocopter to take a fresh

→

look at what had been taken for granted where it related to products, but also to industrial processes.

Thus, we redesigned the whole assembly system for the interior panels, making the operation faster and safer. This earned us the compliments of the workers on the assembly line, whose work was made easier. Design also helped to de-compartmentalize ideas, to imagine transpositions. While someone explained that the glass door model that I proposed (which uses the well known thermoforming technology) was not feasible, I discovered that a similar pane was used on another helicopter model. Yet, it was the same engineer who was working on both models – but projects were too compartmentalized to make an interconnection. Out of the 55 modifications proposed, 50 were accepted. The final product is very faithful to the original concept, which was approved by Hermès' Artistic Director and Eurocopter. For an object of this kind, technical and safety restrictions are obviously primordial. Our innovative work developed from these constraints. In fact, our involvement helped to strengthen the safety of the aircraft – as the head of quality at Eurocopter soon understood. We were instructed to use dark colours in the cockpit to avoid reflected glare from the windows (although the previous VIP version was all in white). This functional limitation dictated the choice of all the colour ranges for the aircraft.

The Hermès helicopter from every angle

Travelling by helicopter gives one the sensation of floating in air: One instinctively seeks to find a point of equilibrium. In the initial version of the aircraft on which we worked, the components of the cockpit were placed asymmetrically, with the impression that the cabin was tilting to one side. The search for a feeling of balance guided our choice while designing the interior, taking care to replace the components in a symmetrical manner. This was even more important since safety depends also on the feeling of being safe in a particular environment.

On the whole, the style of the original helicopter was not very coherent. The components were assembled together in succession,

$\rightarrow$

often with a view to enhancing safety, but without coherence when taken as a whole. That's why we redesigned every detail (handles, safety instructions, etc.). Hermès works as much on the exterior as on the interior of objects. Seeing the helicopter from the outside, one should therefore understand how the space inside is organized.

When you look at the helicopter from the outside, you notice a distinctive Hermès sign – not ostentatious – an orange strip that runs along the length of the aircraft. This graphic touch is not just a simple signature. It is inspired by the wool yarn that pilots sometimes tie to the aircraft to determine, in case of technical failure, whether the helicopter is going up or down. We just created an imaginary prolongation of this yarn around the helicopter. The section that unites the tail and body of the helicopter is very elaborate, with a set of diodes that emit orange light. Seen from outside, the initiated will recognize it as a Hermès helicopter when it descends.

When we looked at the original helicopter, we found that the landing gear was not very functional. Its VIP version consisted of a round tube which was slippery when one placed a foot on it, and the rescue version (for hospitals, mountains) had a flat and functional undercarriage, but not sufficiently appealing for VIP clients. Our work consisted of enhancing its functionality and also the safety and aesthetics of the landing gear.

Our version greatly improves safety and is integrated into the shape of the helicopter. As we mentioned earlier, this innovation delighted Eurocopter.

A space devoted to passengers

Let us now enter the helicopter. We created a panel that separates the cockpit from the passenger area – something that Eurocopter was not in favour of, fearing it would cause vibration. During the first flight, the aircraft provided a feeling of such stability that no one has since mentioned this potential drawback.

$\rightarrow$

We found the space meant for passengers seemed rather restricted. On entering, a passenger would not know where to place his jacket or his briefcase. The space was also encumbered by a bar that could accommodate twenty people, although the cabin holds only four. Some aircrafts were equipped with six television screens, when the average duration of a flight is 40 minutes. One could also assume that the pleasure of a flight consisted more in viewing the landscape than watching a television screen... The passenger cabin that we designed emphasizes horizontal lines to give a sense of space, and therefore of comfort.

We discovered a helicopter of the 1950s later, which used the same principle: this choice was clearly right from a functional standpoint. Wide bench seats accommodate passengers of any corpulence and allow them to stretch their legs. We reduced the bar, made place for a briefcase, created a retractable armrest, under which there is an extinguisher definitely more accessible than in the previous version. The armrest also has a very practical pocket; this solves the problem caused because movement is restricted and it is difficult to reach one's belongings. The principle is that once seated, the traveller has everything he needs within reach.

To make the voyage meaningful, maps and binoculars are available in the cabin. The seats are partly upholstered in leather, but the cabin is mostly covered in fabric, to absorb noise better. Fabric, not considered very luxurious, had never been used in a VIP helicopter. For some of the items, we used a composite that was simply varnished – quite a radical choice for anyone who has a stereotyped view of luxury. While replacing the door handle only worthy of a bathroom that the old model had, we used a carrying handle, very well designed, highly functional and ergonomic. When an object has already been well thought out, why redesign it?

The standard helicopter contained a profusion of rather inelegant safety instruction notices. We created safety notices in the form of labels in a jacquard, similar to clothing labels. They are perhaps not as easily readable as printed labels, but are so beautiful

→

that passengers will certainly pay attention to them – whereas nobody read the stickers before. This is a good illustration of functionality that can also be beautiful.

In the end, when the prototype was presented in Atlanta, visitors told us the helicopter made them "feel at home."

2.3 Manufacturing/workshop talent

- Portrait from a workshop: Madame Jacqueline, *première main d'atelier tailleur* at Chanel Fashion Haute Couture
- Portrait of a founder and independent watchmaker: Max Büsser from MB & Friends
- Four Key Insights: Manufacturing/Workshops in context:
  - The watch manufacturer model
  - The secrets and Savoir-Faire of a high jewelry workshop
  - The story of the Kelly bag
  - How Charles Christofle Built His Brand around Manufacturing

2.3.1 Portrait from a workshop: Madame Jacqueline, Première d'atelier tailleur at Chanel[7]

With her *little hands*, Madame Jacqueline pins a sleeve on the model of a garment she is going to create. From her worktable she oversees the other 50 "petites mains" that are busy preparing for the next fashion show.

She is the première d'atelier tailleur; which grants her the privilege of being called "Madame" followed by her first name.

Dynamic and a perfectionist, her job is to translate Mr. Lagerfeld's sketches into dresses, and to do that as quickly as possible; "if not, it won't be funny" she said.

Madame Jacqueline started with Chanel in 1996, thanks to her enormous passion and love of Haute fashion design. Having graduated from a British fashion school in tailoring, she moved to Paris where she first worked at Guy Laroche (during the Angelo Tarazzi period). She then became première d'atelier at Chloé where she met Karl Lagerfeld, whom she followed when he joined the Chanel team at rue Cambon.

Between the two there is complete trust. "Working for Mr Lagerfeld is a wonderful opportunity; he is a great professional, very skilled and very knowledgeable about clothes. He is always thinking about how to transform his sketches into clothing and provides us with solutions when necessary; and this continuous requirement enables us to grow," she explains.

What does she like most about her job? "Creation, of course; it's rewarding!" Does she have favourite pieces in the Haute Couture collection? "I loved working on a tweed coat with chinchilla accents which belonged to the 2008 Autumn Winter collection ... but for me the next collection always remains the nicest. Starting again from nothing: that is the 'magic' of this job."

2.3.2   Portrait of a founder and independent watchmaker: Max Büsser from MB & Friends

If there is one thing Maximilian Büsser understands completely, **it is the power of collaboration.** Back in 2001, as head of Harry Winston Rare Timepieces, he gathered some of the best designers in the industry to create the Opus series of one-of-a-kind timepieces, transforming the image of the company from diamond merchant to maker of fine horology sought after by collectors.

More remarkable, though, Büsser gave credit where it was due, by putting both the name of the brand and that of the watchmaker alongside the dial and movement. This was something of a breakthrough in the watch world, where companies prefer to highlight the brand name and downplay the designers behind their products.

Now Büsser, 44, is doing it again with his own brand, MB&F (Maximilian Büsser & Friends), which he set up in 2005 with 700,000 Swiss francs, or $630,000, from his savings. As a business model, Büsser is borrowing what the Swiss watchmaker Abraham-Louis Breguet did 200 years before: selling products based on their design and asking for down payments from retailers to complete the work. Büsser has secured orders from six retailers willing to pay 35 percent upfront.

MB&F is producing limited editions of highly innovative watches that Büsser calls Horological Machines, "because that's simply what they are." The new watch called The Legacy Machine 1 is a kind of homage to "old school" watchmaking. As Büsser explains "Everything on this watch was created with craftsmanship and technology that existed over the 150 years ago. The movement was designed by Kari Voutilainen who is *the* specialist of nineteenth century watchmaking. And Jean-François Mojon who worked on the Opus 10 engineered the movement."

To Büsser, bringing the design talent out of the backroom and into the spotlight is simply good business. "All these people are usually unsung heroes working for other brands," he said. "For them and for me it's a win-win situation, because it's the first time that their names appear somewhere, so they're going to give it their best." For instance, the LM1 was three and a half years in the making and involved approximately 45 people.

Of German-Swiss and Indian parentage, Büsser was born in Italy and raised in Switzerland, where he studied microtechnology at the Swiss Federal Institute of Technology, Lausanne. His career in watchmaking started by chance: In 1991, on a ski vacation in Verbier, Switzerland, he bumped into Henry-John Belmont, managing director of the then-ailing watchmaker Jaeger-LeCoultre, whom Büsser had interviewed as part of a university project. Though he was waiting to hear about a marketing job at Nestlé, Büsser joked with Belmont: "If I don't get it, give me a job." A week later, Belmont did.

One of Büsser's early coups was pushing hard for Jaeger-LeCoultre's first diamond-set watch in 1994, after noticing that Asprey, the upscale London jeweler, was selling many such watches by other makers, to its clients. Within three years, diamond watches represented 25 percent of Jaeger-LeCoultre's revenue.

Recruited in 1998 to head Harry Winston's watch division, Büsser set about invigorating what was at the time a sleepy sideline to the famed New York jeweler's business. Büsser overhauled the supply chain and transformed the handicap of being a limited-outlet retailer into a marketing advantage by stressing the "rarity" of its pieces. When Büsser left Harry Winston in 2005, the watch division had grown from 7 employees to 80, and revenue had grown 900 percent to around $70 million.

But the more Harry Winston grew, the less Büsser enjoyed the work. "I realized the start-up mentality was what I missed most," he said.

Today, Büsser is projecting growth that will "stabilize" at 12 million to 15 million CHF a year. "I want to keep the company small" he said.

As a matter of coincidence, on the very same day that MB&F launched its Legacy Machine N°1, the doors of its first ever concept store in Geneva flew open. Better known as the M.A.D Gallery, this was no simple boutique, but a thoughtfully curated exhibition space housing the complete range of Horological Machines which rub shoulders with a variety of "art" machines created by designers from across the globe.[8]

2.3.3   Four key insights: manufacturing/workshops in context

The following four studies further illustrate the elements that characterize the particular landscape the manufacturer/ workshop and challenges. Instead of describing specific profiles – as we did in the first three parts – we will focus here on the importance of the craftsmanship and its related "savoir faire" or know-how.

- **Key Insight 1** will look at the watch workshop model and related skills.
- **Key Insight 2** will of the High Jewelry workshops' "métiers" and true "savoir faire" – and introduces us to the characteristics of craftsmen.
- **Key Insight 3** describes how a luxury brand (Hermès) builds itself around craftsmanship: the Kelly bag case.
- **Key Insight 4** describes how a luxury brand (Christofle) built itself around manufacturing.

Insight 1: The watch manufacturer model

Figure 2.12 discloses the watch making traditions and skills that brands and groups wish to preserve and to develop.

"Philosophy"	"Skills"
Fine watch making stands at the apex of art and technology	Numerous specialists bring their skills to the creation of a mechanical movement: designers, engineers, draftsmen, past-makers, digital machine operators, metallurgist, chemists, technicians, watchmakers specialising in assembling, adjusting, testing and finishing and master watchmakers whose task is to develop sophisticated mechanical "complications"
Is the sum of dozens of highly skilled professionals and generations of expertise	
Once spread among countless workshops, all these skills are now brought together under a single roof at the workshop or factory	Alongside them work craftsmen whose expertise is equally precious and diverse. Stylists, prototype-makers, makers of cases, dials and hands, polishers, bevellers, engine, tuners, engravers, jewellers, gemmologists and stone-setters,... all contribute to making the fine watch a rare and unique object which as well as "keeping time" celebrates its beauty and mystery
Watchmakers who produce the mechanical movements, and craftsmen who imagine, create and decorate the watch's exterior, work hand-in-hand towards the same creative goal	

"History & Tradition"

Each watch Manufacturer cherishes is own culture, derived from its history, its discoveries and its tradition, often centuries-old

Thanks to the combination of knowledge passed down through generations and the most advanced technology of today, the Manufacturer is now able to create the most sophisticated and most accurate timepieces ever in the history of time measurement

Figure 2.12   The watch manufacturer model: a concentration of skills

Insight 2: The secrets and Savoir-Faire of a high jewelry workshop

The very secretive world of jewelry production

We are somewhere in Paris, close to the Place Vendôme, where the very essence of jewelry resides through the best and well known jewelers.

A meeting is arranged with the head of one of the original High Jewelry Workshops to talk about this fascinating world. The purpose of our interview is to better understand the essence of its unique creation: The best kept secrets, the unique Savoir-Faire and some insights about managing a team of highly skilled craftsmen.

Excerpts from our conversation

"Only the best of the craftsmen can lead the High Jewelry workshop team. His credibility and talent must be acknowledged and accepted by all the people he is working with in the atelier."

"the mission and responsibility of the workshop leader is to inspire passion and trust. Besides overseeing all of the workshop's creations he also supervises each stage of each pieces' operations."

"the workshop's creation is the amount of work that goes into crafting (up to 1500 man hours just for one piece) and a great discipline among the team craftsmanship (each piece is crafted by an individual team member – with the help, if necessary, of the workshop leader – expert among experts and recognized as such by his team) to deliver an art masterpiece on schedule ... There is no way to be late for a particular birthday or a great business event."

"In the workshop the right gesture is critical ... it's crucial to do it once and to do it nice ... a second try is impossible."

$\rightarrow$

"a jewel is a very particular object ... beyond the value of the metal and the stones with which it is made, it carries within itself the Human Genius ... one eye and two hands."

"**traditional tools:** wire-cutter, hammer, pliers ... and common techniques: felting, grinding, lapping, sawing etc. are always used (the same for the last two centuries) as well as true **modern technological** innovations: laser, CAO, 3D ... which enables refinements to some of the design of the jewelry pieces."

"**the apprenticeship model** is the unique way to learn and to transfer the subtle combination of Savoir-Faire, design, and mystery about jewelry creation."

"these are ancestral skills passed on from generation to generation during demanding apprenticeships ... that require 15 to 20 years to become an acknowledged master."

"the key point of the workshop is to maintain and preserve the mythical mystery of setting jewels."

"The final result for the client is an art masterpiece of precious stone in a piece of jewelry with no visible setting ... it's a extraordinary experience for him /her to feel the effect of all the richness of this profession of crafting Art."

"He/she often say: **I didn't see anything** – which is a great accolade for the workshop team's craftsmanship."

The High Jewelry Workshop's *métiers* and *savoir faire*

There are a wide range of specific trades and crafts – *métiers* – in a High Jewelry Workshop. All of them require a professional certificate of capacity (delivered by accredited and academic schools in France, Switzerland and the United States, among others) and/ or a degree or higher-education qualification. In addition, a long and patient apprenticeship in a workshop, close to a Master, is the unique way to practice the right gesture and learn to be rigorous and methodical, showing attention to detail.

$\rightarrow$

Below are some of the key high jewelry "métiers" working in a workshop or "atelier"[9], each of whom maintains and preserves the specific skills and the mythical mystery to designing jewelry.

The gemologist

The Gemologist buys precious stones and checks their quality, which he/she confirms by issuing quality control certificates. He/she registers and labels the gemstones to guarantee their traceability during the manufacturing phase.

He/she is constantly aware of the status of his/her stock of gems. The gemologist is also required to manage and supervise the re-cutting of gems.

The gem-cutter (or lapidary)

The gem-cutter cuts or re-cuts gems according to the task at hand, under the supervision of the gemologist.

He or she guarantees the final look of a precious stone, while respecting its geometry and following precise instructions. Sawing, grinding, sanding lapping drilling are some of the operations that he/she must master.

The gem-setter

Only the gem-setter understands how to combine precious or semi-precious stones with metal in a harmonious manner. Patient and meticulous, the gem-setter knows how to give watches and jewelry that extra sparkle by inserting diamonds, rubies or emeralds.

He/she coordinates the arrangement of gems so that they reflect a maximum of light. He/she can also restore pieces where needed.

$\rightarrow$

The polisher

The polisher prepares his/her tools according to the task. He/she creates the final look of a piece, while respecting its geometry and following precise instructions. Felting, satin-brushing, micro-beading and grinding are some of the operations that he/she must master in order to transform dull and gloomy elements into shiny objects that reflect light.

The jeweler

The jeweler knows how to enhance a stone or a set of precious stones sitting on a framework of noble metal. He/she begins by making sketches of the piece of jewelry before actually proceeding with its creation. The jeweler is often called upon to create pieces that will be produced in limited quantities or even as a unique, single creation.

What craftsmanship is all about

Luxury does not exist without craftsmen. The previous description of what happens in a jewelry workshop can be replicated in any Haute Couture atelier, in a porcelain factory or in a leather-goods workshop. A recent Hermès movie[10] depicting all its *métiers* through the craftsmen and craftswomen that embody them is living proof of their importance throughout the industry.

Craftsmen are specialized experts. Experts have been extremely well characterized by Goery Delacôte[11] as follows:

Imagine you have a chessboard with a game that is in progress. The chessboard is covered and then briefly shown to two different people: a chess novice (like most of us) and an expert. You then ask them to describe the board: the novice will get two out of ten pieces right and the expert nine out of ten! The difference? The novice sees the board as a random positioning of pieces. The expert sees it as a game which he or she has seen before. The

$\rightarrow$

expert can even tell you what the previous moves were and what the subsequent moves will be. The reason for this extraordinary insight is that experts have, over time, developed a visual memory of tens of thousands of games and possible positions on the board. The expert will see a situation within a game where the novice will only see individual pieces not related one to another. The expert can therefore identify and select relevant information to solve a problem.

Managing a team of experts needs very specific competencies since each expert craftsman will only be motivated by passion or the furthering of his expertise, and will only recognize authority derived from a similar expertise. Out of the three possible ways a workshop leader[12] could be given that title (being identified by the hierarchy/having moved up the ranks/being a Master among peers) only last one is probable in a craftsmanship setting: the Head of the Atelier will be self-evident, respected for his or her skill and talent.

Insight 3: The story of the Kelly bag[13]

How it began

In 1892, Hermès created a plain saddlebag designed for hunters. In 1930 a smaller version for ladies was created by Robert Dumas as a limited edition. It was simply called "sac a courroies pour dames" meaning a bag with straps for ladies. As it happens, in 1956 LIFE magazine featured on its cover a portrait of Grace Kelly holding the bag, a large-size one made of crocodile skin, allegedly to cover her pregnancy. The 1954-Oscar winner had recently been married (in April 1956) to prince Rainier of Monaco.

It took an American princess and a magazine cover to propel the bag to superstardom. This picture was featured in the press around the world and turned the bag into an overnight sensation.

→

It was immediately renamed The Kelly by fashion trend makers, but it took 21 years for the house of Hermès to do so officially.

The craftsmanship behind the Kelly

In the Hermès workshops: Did you know that a Kelly bag is made by a single craftsman at Hermès? Every year the company buys hundreds of animal skins for its 12 production sites, all based in France. The most precious skins are handled in Pantin (in the outskirts of Paris) and in the specialist workshop on rue du Faubourg Saint Honoré in central of Paris. Figure 2.13 hints at the craftsmanship behind the Kelly bag.

Figure 2.13   The craftsmanship behind the Kelly bag

→

Preparing the skins: There are more than 20 standardized steps in the transformation of animal skin into a bag, and almost 200 different techniques including plucking, gumming, smoothing, thinning down, treating and massaging with the firm objective of making that skin completely smooth.

The cutting workshop: Here each piece of skin is numbered before being pieced together with the other parts that make up a bag. Three skins are required to make one Kelly bag – because only the perfect parts of each skin are used.

Precious skins: Each bag is made by one craftsman only. The work required one precious skin such as crocodile, ostrich, and lizard skin is all handled by a single experienced craftsman.

Features of the Kelly bag: Aside from its trapezoid shape, the rigid bottom that stands on four metallic studs, its flaps, its triangular gussets and its curved, sculpted handle, the other features that identify a Kelly bag are the straps that cross over the clasp, the padlock and the little bell that protects the key.

Signature: All this work is performed with care, patience and love by a craftsman who takes around 20 hours to sew, stitch, glue and assemble the 36 pieces of leather that make up a Kelly bag, before adding his personal signature (to identify the craftsman that created it – who will take charge of the bag if and when it comes in for repairs).

Insight 4: How Charles Christofle built his brand around manufacturing[14]

Christofle, known today as one of the world's leading silverware brands, was named for Charles Christofle who, in 1831, headed a small jewelry workshop. The story of the company's creation is that of his dream: to move out of craftsmanship and into industry. He always saw himself as more of an entrepreneur,

→

heading a company, than a craftsman. This was a completely new attitude for the early nineteenth century. How did he manage to build it into a success? The answer lies in his vision: He was both a manufacturer and a businessman.

The manufacturer

Charles Christofle was constantly looking for innovative processes that could simplify production. His masterstroke came in 1842, when he bought the rights to a recent patent on electrolytic plating. Gold and silver plating were very dangerous at the time: It made use of mercury and nitric acid that killed workers. Use of electricity was a major breakthrough, both for health reasons and for business reasons since plating could now be done on an industrial scale.

Christofle believed in research and in the application of scientific discoveries to industry. He therefore hired engineers to research aluminum and alloys and kept close contact with leading French and British scientists of his time.

Since he wasn't being supplied with the top quality products that he hoped to be plated, he decided to venture into the goldsmith and silversmith trade himself. His aim was to control the all aspects of production so that his master's stamp could guarantee the final product (and not, as was the tradition, non-plated objects only).

In 1848, the company was given the title "Manufacture d'orfèvrerie" (silversmith workshop) which proved his point.

The businessman

Charles Christofle had a very innovative business sense. In fact, he created a whole new market in that, before him, the silver plate market was nonexistent. He had the intuition that these new products, manufactured industrially but with a master goldsmith's stamp, would become luxury items for the new and fast developing industrial bourgeoisie, as opposed to the

→

traditional gold and sterling ware who was the privilege of aristocracy. The bourgeoisie was all about appearances; the table was its focal point for social gatherings and the table needed to be dressed with beautiful silver pieces.

He had some of the top artists and designers work for him which allowed him to price his pieces accordingly.

He also was convinced that his markets lay beyond France and was one of the first to export his products. He built his global reputation through Universal Exhibitions, using it both as a distribution channel and a privileged method for building brand awareness. His channels of distribution were a mix of Christofle stores – mainly used as showrooms – and selected boutiques.

Faced with lower quality products that began to flood the market he created a "manufacturing brand" which acted as a personal signature and allowed him to guarantee his customers the highest quality. This quality, and the guarantee that goes along with it, enabled Charles Christofle to sell his products at very high prices and use the margin to finance the development of the company.

2.4   Retail talent

- A retail portrait: Marc Auclert – from a collection of stones to *Maison Auclert*
- Three retail job descriptions:
  - Store Director
  - Sales Staff
  - Sales Experts/"Grand Vendeur"
- Three key insights: retail talent in context
  - Shop responsibilities
  - A retail career path example
  - What you need to know about Sales Experts/"Grand Vendeur"

2.4.1 A retail portrait: Marc Auclert[15]

From a stone collection to Maison Auclert

It all began with a young boy's collection collection of stones, crystals and pebbles that, as a child, Marc Auclert sought for their shape, colour and brilliance. Even while studying economics and politics at the renowned IEP in Paris, Marc Auclert never lost his childhood passion and continued to look for stones in his spare time. He came to understand what really mattered to him in life, and realized that his destiny was to deal with stones.

His mother being English, he ventured to New York where he registered at the Gemmological Institute of America and graduated: The key to his new life. Marc Auclert then came back to Paris where he learned the trade among Place Vendôme's "grands vendeurs" at Chaumet. Charming and a good people-reader with great communication skills, he was sent him back to New York by Chaumet to open and manage a corner at Saks Fifth Avenue. This experience in business development was soon followed by others: at Chanel for seven years to launch the jewelry business, then for two years at Sotheby's *Diamonds in London* to set up their retail activity, and then, from 2007 to 2009, at De Beers Diamond Jeweler in Tokyo as CEO Asia.

Without a doubt, Marc Auclert's first-hand retail knowledge was a strong asset throughout his career. But what may have made an even greater difference are the qualities – tenacity and vision – that he had developed long ago as a collector of stones, since those are the same qualities one needs to be a good business developer.

Today – among other projects and activities – this curious mind, grandson of a Paris antique dealer, hunts antique gems and ornaments all over the world. He selects them not only for their beauty and preciousness but also for the poetry of their history. He then has them reset on modern settings and, as a proof of authenticity, sells them under his very own name; through the label "Maison Auclert."

Lesson learnt

By melding heritage-infused pieces with modernity and proposing meaningful jewels, Marc Auclert reminds us of the quintessence of luxury: One needs to know where he comes from to understand where his path has led him today. Once again – as in the portraits of luxury leaders – we recognize the importance of a person's cultural heritage and background when building our understanding of what makes a successful leader in the luxury industry.

2.4.2 Three retail job descriptions

The retail population is usually the largest in a luxury brand's origination. Of the various retail job possibilities, the following

	Store Director
Role	• **Optimization of store's commercial performance** Responsible for increasing sales and reaching commercial objectives set by HQ Guarantee the quality of client service in accordance with company's policies Manage the P&L of the store regarding running expenses and budget control • **Management of the store team** Motivate store team and ensures the organization of team tasks Oversee the quality of the sales staff trough recruitment, training, evaluation and development • **Daily management of operations** Assume all management responsibilities of store (stock, accounts, sales, etc) Maintain high quality standards in store (customer services, in-store merchandising, administration and storage areas)
Skills	• **Capacity to manage retail performance that enhances revenues while controlling costs and shrinkage** • **Ability to manage staff: recruit, train, motivate and retain productive team** • **Excellent communication and customer service skills**
Behavior	• **Higher "education" with a passion to represent a luxury brand as an ambassador** • **Talent to forge strong diverse teams** • **Keen sense for following the luxury goods market trends**
Experience required	• **Bachelor degree and minimum 5 years of retail experience or significant experience as an Assistant Store Manager** • **English compulsory. Foreign language a plus**

Figure 2.14 Store Director job description

roles provide a good illustration of what this population's activities and behaviors: Store Director, Sales Staff and Sales Expert.

The Store Director

He or she heads a small business unit with a trained and motivated sales team. Using their acute sales and social skills, they must create a pleasurable experience for each and every customer that shops in the store (see Figure 2.14).

The Sales Staff

As a member of the store's team, he or she is required to deliver a unique shopping experience to the clientele in-line with the

---

Sales Staff

Role	• **Develop sales in order to meet commercial targets** Responsible for selling directly to all customer categories Responsible for increasing sales and encouraging brand loyalty • **Understand and explain the craftsman experience** Apply product information and sales arguments in accordance with company policy Ensure optimum stock levels to reach objectives • **Establish a good relationship with clients** Keep client files up to date Encourage customer loyalty through good communication, service and personal contact
Skills	• **Strong sense of negotiation to reach commercial targets with efficiency, having a constructive attitude and approach** • **Deep understanding for handling client complains with calm and diplomacy** • **Professional ability to create value through quality service** • **Ability to maintain energy and focus**
Behavior	• **Passion and inspiration to sell crafted product** • **A keen sense for "intimacy" and "intercultural particularities" regarding sales attitude** • **Strong curiosity for following luxury goods market trends**
Experience required	• **Bachelor's degree** • **English compulsory, Russian or Mandarin a plus**

Figure 2.15 Sales Staff job description

brand's strategy, in order to maximize sales and establish long term customer relationships (see Figure 2.15).

The Sales Expert

Focused on high ticket sales, this individual acts like more like a "concierge" than a sales person by advising clients, not just on their purchase, but also in whatever other matters using his/her well-developed personal network (see Figure 2.16).

"Developing Customer Service" in Part 4 of this book will delve further into the realm of retail. In it, we will look at specific approaches to key retail challenges such as "talent retail diagnosis" and use some tools from The Managing Toolbox[16] regarding retail recruitment, retail career development and retail compensation systems.

	Sales Expert-Grand Vendeur
Role	• **Develop exceptional sales in order to achieve commercial target** Responsible for selling directly to high level clientele Participate in special sales events as a brand ambassador • **Represent and explain the craftsman experience** Apply product and sales arguments in accordance with company policy Ensure optimum stock levels to reach objectives • **Develop and maintain strong relationship with high level clientele** Use relationship network strategically to deliver sales and services Keep client files up to date
Skills	• **Willingness to sell directly to high level clientele categories** • **Exceptional negotiation abilities in order win in seemingly impossiblesituations** • **Capacity to follow his /her business instincts in situations where there is no way of being certain of the outcomes**
Behavior	• **A strong and forceful personality with a smooth, enticing and elegant style** • **Confidence to deal with "high ticket sales"** • **Drive to be #1**
Experience required	• **A strong client network at high levels that pay off** • **A proven sales track record**

Figure 2.16 Sales Expert job description

2.4.3 Three key insights: sales talent in context

The following combination of scenarios and observations provide further insights into the retail population and function.

- **Insight 1** describes at how stores are best presented as business units.
- **Insight 2** follows a model retail career path and identifies key lessons learned.
- **Insight 3** looks at the "Grands Vendeur" population and provides valuable tips for those who manage them.

Insight 1: The shop as a business unit

Successful luxury brands treat each of their stores as a business unit, with a skilled professional at the head of a team of motivated and trained sales people. Viewing a store as a business unit requires a clear understanding of its main responsibilities (see Figure 2.17)

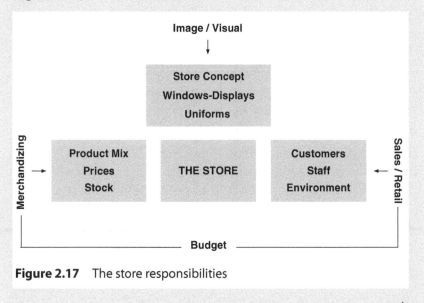

Figure 2.17   The store responsibilities

→

For a luxury brand, everything that concerns merchandising and brand image falls under the remit of the Creative Director (and the Head of Visual Merchandising); product mix and prices are determined by central teams (Merchandising Director and their team) while the budget is defined by the Finance Department. The only domain left under the direct responsibility of the store team is sales itself; managing customers and managing the relationship with the store's environment. This is where a significant difference can be made by a good store manager: Managing and training the sales team, managing customer relationships at store level (and within the corporate CRM system, if one exists) and being a local brand ambassador.

Insight 2: A retail career path example

Shu L, a Chinese woman from Honk Kong, grew up in a well-educated and trade-oriented environment between Honk Kong, Paris and London, where the family business dealing in the trade and sales of Chinese Art has locations.

Shu L. has achieved a relevant and interesting luxury career path; people who know her say she is "a very hard working girl with taste for challenges and success"

Figure 2.18 shows the different major steps of her retail career path: Her international profile and early experience with the family business in a marketing and communication role allowed her to be selected for a Luxury Brand Management MBA in Paris. Thanks to this diploma, she landed a first job in a Luxury Group for a jewelry brand, where she was responsible for dealing with customer complaints as an After Sales Manager.

$\rightarrow$

After this valuable but demanding experience, she moved within the group to a fashion brand that offered her a position as Sales Manager in the Milan Flagship. In order to learn the all necessary procedures relative to the fashion industry she attended a summer program with the Istituto Marangoni Design School in Milan. Her success in both management and customer relationships enabled her to be appointed to a higher and critical position as Responsible for the VIP clientele.

In 2006, the fashion brand's expansion and development in Asia needed native Chinese candidates: this gave her the opportunity to get a management position as Store Director in Hong Kong. Today she is Retail Director for the Chinese market where she is learning, alongside the Italian country manager, her role as ambassador of the brand.

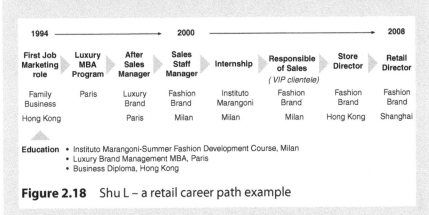

Figure 2.18   Shu L – a retail career path example

The four lessons to be learned from this career development example

- Her family's trade and international values helped her be comfortable in the luxury business sector.
- Her decision to seek international luxury business diplomas and get targeted internship experience with diverse luxury brands (jewelry, then fashion) were the way for her to figure out how things work in the luxury industry.

$\rightarrow$

- The expertise she built in retail, step by step, including sales proficiency, store and team management plus client services in both European and Asian markets provided her with a significant advantage.
- The fact she seized a challenging opportunity of a leadership role in the Chinese market, close to a trusted mentor, demonstrates that staying in touch after her first experience in Italy has paid off.

Insight 3: How to lead Sales Experts or "Grands Vendeurs"

Luxury jewelry brands have developed a unique sales channel that other categories do not share: Men and women capable of handling one-to-one sales with VIP clients. Based on numerous interviews of Sales Experts or "Grands Vendeurs," we have established a list of six common characteristics of the individuals within this population which collectively make them a difficult crew to manage[17] and of which their leaders need to be aware:

1. **They know their worth**; and know that if they move, their knowledge and network move with them.
2. **They are persistent and compulsive**; they have an enormous amount of energy and willpower and are driven by an obsession to make outstanding deals.
3. **They are well connected**; they continuously network with their extremely wealthy clients; these networks increase their value to the organization.
4. **They ignore corporate hierarchies**; they are autonomous and independent, daring to be different; they do not feel a need to fit-in.

5. **They expect instant access;** if they can't access their CEO directly, they may think the organization doesn't value them – and could walk out the door!
6. **They crave recognition**

Yves Saint Laurent and Pierre Bergé: a successful leadership duo

Case studies

Introduction

Part 3 of this book has three objectives:

Use real examples to learn how to anticipate and tackle some of the luxury industry's idiosyncrasies described in the two first chapters: corporate culture, the family business system, the creative element and leadership

Highlight critical people, change leadership issues: to anticipate and to prepare succession planning, to behave appropriately to fit with a very tribal corporate culture, adopt the "can do" attitude when necessary, etc.

Understand how to cope with the luxury culture experience

The four following case studies all focus on change management issues with a strong people dimension:

Case study 1: The Robert Polet Case is about the integration of an "outsider" in a new and specific internal corporate culture – and the leadership style he used to manage a complex luxury group.

Case study 2: The Family Business Case reveals succession issues within a family business system; an important concern in the luxury industry.

Case study 3: Moving from Marketing to Creation illustrates the very complex career path of a Creative, coming from the US, in a famous centenary luxury brand.

Case study 4: The Dior Leadership Duo provides the common factors that a well-known leadership duo developed to succeed.

We will look at each case studies in the following format:

- Biography, background and key facts about the business situation
- Tangible outcomes achieved by the leader/ manager where appropriate
- Focus on the Manager/Leader's leadership style including personal touch, traits and temperaments
- Key lessons

3.1   Case study 1: Robert Polet, a "modern gipsy at Gucci"[1]

3.1.1   Background and professional biography

Rober Polet is a Dutch national. Born in 1955 in Malaysia, he was educated in the Netherlands and in Britain and received his MBA diploma at the University of Oregon in the United States.

He started his professional career in a marketing position at Unilever and essentially "grew up" in the group, rising to a broad range of management roles and geographic responsibilities which saw him move 11 times throughout the world, with postings that included Amsterdam, Brussels, Hamburg, Hong Kong, Kuala Lumpur, London, Milan and Paris.

His last management role at Unilever was CEO of "Ice Cream and Frozen Foods."

In July 2004, he joined Gucci Group as Chairman and CEO.

3.1.2 The challenges at Gucci in 2004

The departures of Tom Ford (Artistic Director) and Domenico De Sole (Executive Chairman) – Gucci's Dream Team – raised the critical question of who could run the Gucci corporate strategy?

As usual in such a change situation, several insiders predicted that Tom Ford's departure would spell the end of Gucci. Besides, with the exception of Gucci, most Gucci Group brands were losing money.

The PPR decision was to recruit from outside the luxury industry. The brief given to the headhunter regarding the new CEO of Gucci Group stated that they were *"looking for someone with international experience above all and a strong track record on managing brands and a group of brands."*

A few months later, Robert Polet – the "ice cream man" from Unilever – was appointed; a choice that was considered a risky bet for the Gucci group by many luxury industry professionals.

3.1.3 His main achievement as Gucci Group Chairman and CEO

Thanks to his previous management experience, Polet gets off to a fast start, taking a short integration period to get to know the people involved and to understand the key business drivers that enable him to promote his strong beliefs:

His first assertion was to put the brand over the designer:

> *"The brand is always more important than the designer because the brand will stay with us, and with your children and our children's children out into infinity"*

In-line with his statement, he moved the organization's focus away from personalities towards the brands themselves. He gave each brand direct control over its own label and required each brand's CEO to submit a three-year business plan every year.

Regarding the Gucci brand, a plan was put forward to double its sales over the next seven years to 3 billions €.

He then, selected creative directors who shared his philosophy and were more passionate about the product than about potential celebrity: Fridda Gianini for Gucci, Tomas Maier for Bottega Venetta. He also pushed through the complete integration of the Stella McCartney brand.

Likewise he encouraged "a culture of interchange" among brands, geographies and management levels; established quarterly management committee meetings, annual leadership conferences for the Top 200 managers and a variety of experience-sharing meetings for other functional experts.

As the result, several brands including Bottega Veneta, Alexander McQueen and Stella McCartney posted positive incomes for the first time in 2007; thanks to these impressive results, Fortune named Robert Polet "Europe Businessman of the Year" for 2007.

But in the beginning of 2011, a surprise reorganization led by François-Henri Pinault, the owner of the PPR SA and Gucci's parent, pushed him to leave the company after seven years as a CEO. At that point in time, some of the ambitious targets he set to expand the company has been met, such as:

- Giving the Group's eight luxury brands more autonomy;
- Increasing margins;
- Making smaller brands like Alexander McQueen and Stella McCartney profitable;
- Pushing Bottega Venetta sales to be a strong N°2 in the luxury portfolio after Gucci;
- Delivering a substantial net profit to PPR SA, Gucci parent.

Following his departure, the role has ceased to exist and the Gucci Group banner has disappeared, becoming PPR's "Luxury Business Group", the CEO of which will report directly to PPR Chairman and CEO François-Henri Pinault.

In August 2011, SAFILO, the N° 2 Eyewear maker (with brands such as Carrera and licensed branded collections for Giorgio

Armani, Gucci and other fashion labels) appointed Robert Polet as Chairman.

3.1.4   Four lessons to learn from an outsider in the luxury industry

Lesson 1: The Gucci Group was ready to **welcome an "outsider"** as a leader coming from another industry in 2004; the Group sought a leader with strong marketing and management skills capable of bringing a fresh approach to managing its brands and its people while attracting a new generation of managers and focusing attention on the customer experience.

Lesson 2: Robert Polet is a global leader with a **strong cultural and family background and an international education.**

His early international exposure allowed him to develop a keen sense of understanding for cross cultural nuances. These helped him be recognized as a true leader by his managers and designers who came from all over the world.

Likewise, his early career challenges at Unilever, where he moved 11 times from Europe to Asia and the USA, gave him a natural cultural empathy and a great sense of leadership.

His extensive experience in tackling challenging foreign assignments helped him be effective and relevant in its first analysis and decision for the Gucci Group.

Last but not least, the cultural openness of his family (spouse and children) and their successful adaptation of global lifestyles is one of his key success factors in his career development.

Lesson 3: Polet is a leader with **strong Emotional Intelligence skills.**

He is able to trust his executives – *"with Robert if you have a problem, you pick up a bag and go to Italy and work it out yourself"*

As he is proactive and truly creative himself, he is very comfortable with the creatives and designers he works with.

He is very effective in his way of leading people, espousing ideas like *"the art of letting go"* and the freedom *"to Break the rules"* as some of his management principles. Polet led the Gucci Group with a light HQ (limited to HR, Finance and Operations) and made regular visits to all the brands, to making them feel "empowered and accountable" in order to cope with change and function under the pressure.

Finally, he is a man at peace with himself; his healthy narcissism allowing him to stay positive when he was mocked as the *"Ice cream man"* by all the luxury "experts."

Lesson 4: Each brand has its DNA and heritage – and they are to be respected with humility.

One of Robert Polet's major traits as CEO of the Gucci Group was, according to the Managing Director of one of the business units reporting to him, *"to switch with great ease from one brand to another"* and *"to give each CEO complete autonomy in managing and developing his brand."*

Too many executives will have a very hands-on attitude and, thinking their past successful experience is a proof of their know-how, will try to impose their views when entering a luxury brand. Robert Polet is living proof of a very different attitude: he would openly question the strategies of each brand and enter an iterative process with his team members, thereby leading each CEO to come up with the best possible answers. Coming from outside the luxury industry he could adapt to every single brand and promote the very best executives to top positions.

3.2   Case Study 2: A difficult succession plan in a family luxury business

3.2.1   The situation at the Company in 2000

We are somewhere in Paris, with a family business that's been around for over 100 years. It is profitable, its business performances are excellent and there's a long-term vision for the brand.

The company has a wide product portfolio including leather, clothes, perfume and watches. More than 6000 people work for the company worldwide, many in the factory and special workshops that are still based in France.

When you meet the family business board members they talk about:

> *"a brand synonymous of very high quality; a well recognized craftsmanship experience with a willingness to maintain and develop its concentration of skills and savoir-faire in France and Switzerland for the watches."*

> *"the strong family business pact that is the core business model; the family owns the majority of the total shares."*

It is time for the family to prepare the succession. The current CEO (a family member) is seeking his successor; he would prefer to find someone within the family ... but despite his great efforts this option doesn't work. An international search firm is required to help him in this difficult issue.

Early in 2000, thanks to the support of the headhunter, a new CEO is finally hired. The CEO splits his global role in creation and business development into two new ones:

• An Artistic role for a family member.
• An International Strategy Development function for a VP who would come from outside the family business.

3.2.2 Background and professional biography of the new VP

The new VP is 38 years old. He is French.

A graduate from a French business diploma (Grande Ecole) he gained an outstanding fast-track career path within a major player in the consumer goods industry where he has successfully managed key responsibilities in marketing development and brand leadership.

He joined the company in 2000 as VP International Strategic Development.

3.2.3   Clues for understanding why the succession was difficult

The lack of agreement between the family's key members and the Board regarding the communication strategy regarding the succession was damaging to the process.

The new VP received a Letter of Mission: *"Do nothing during your first hundred days... just see and learn"* which could both represent:

- An exceptional opportunity to acquire and understand the specifics of the corporate and brand culture: rituals, expected behaviors, respective roles and vision of the world.
- A trap for someone new to the luxury environment with a marketing background from a risk taking professional culture.

Therefore, the position of the CEO, being both chairman and a family member, adds a political complexity and challenges to the newcomer.

> *"His entrepreneurial and inspired family guide role became a legend within the Brand – that made people feel he was unique and not replaceable."*

Some of the key senior managers didn't believe on his leaving at all. Likewise, his strong presence in the transition phase has disturbed the brand continuity.

In addition, the newcomer made some critical mistakes relative to the expected behavior that nurtured anger, fear and rejection.

- His willingness to manage the Brand communication, as he used to do in his previous positions, conflicted with the habits in the luxury industry where this matter is the "reserved domain" of the CEO. This has disturbed the perception key family members and shareholders had of him.

- His desire to create his "own legend" through very quick organization and people changes – the opposite of the letter of mission purpose – created a negative connection between him and the employees and accelerated his isolation.

As the result, the succession has ended before the first year of collaboration. A former and respected Senior Manager has been recalled to fill the position.

3.2.4 Four lessons to learn from a succession in a luxury family business

What needs to be done to achieve a balance between the emotions that inevitability surround the succession process and the commercial interests of the business and its prospects for success?

Lesson 1: Appoint a facilitator who can support the global operation.

This individual may be a widely accepted family member, a member of the company advisory board, or some other external adviser in whom the owners have confidence.

Lesson 2: View **succession planning as a process**, not a traditional "rat race."

There are four key general phases to plan carefully in the CEO – led succession process as can be seen in Figure 3.1.

In addition to this professional process, it is vital to take into account three factors:

- The current and future ownership structure: Is ownership in the hands of one individual, a manageable group of close relatives, such as cousins or a sprawling family dynasty? What impact will a generational shift have on this structure?
- The investment structure: Is the company a focused or a diversified family business? What are the family's intentions for the future?

Phase 1 Situation assessment	Phase 2 Engagement	Phase 3 Search/selection	Phase 4 Transition
Timing	Board/Family engagement	Search for external candidates	Communication
Development of selection criteria	Agreement on selection criteria	Development of selection criteria	Overlap period
Identification of internal candidates including family members	Internal communication strategy	Assessment of internal and external candidates	First hundred days for new CEO
Development plans for andidates	Involvement of others stakeholders	Recommendation to Board/Family	"Old CEO" moves or leads a transition role
Board/Famil engagement		Final selection	

Figure 3.1   The succession process in a family business

- The governance structure: Is the business owner-managed, family managed, overseen by the family or externally managed?

Search experts estimate that the cost of a failed hire is at least four times salary and bonus (source: Heidrick & Struggles)

Lesson 3: Split responsibilities
Formally, the Board and the key family members own the succession decision while the CEO, with the assistance of the external advisor, should manage the succession process.

Lesson 4: Master the **Emotional Ownership** that is unique to family business.

The outgoing CEO must be able **to manage the complex and often frustrating politics and emotions** that surface. To handle that carefully, the CEO has to:

- Earn political support by dealing with factions within the board, avoiding destructive internal politics and by balancing needs for external constituencies.
- Leave room for emotion by addressing personal emotions, helping those not selected to adjust and creating support for the new CEO.
- Move on, when appropriate.[2]

3.3   Case Study 3: From marketing development to creation

3.3.1   The situation at the Company in 2000

In 2000 this Luxury Brand was a worldwide leader in jewelry, watches and a significant force in accessories. In this challenging business, the new CEO of the brand wanted to attract international creative talents with a strong professional background in fashion and accessories.

The CEO, being aware of the challenges of integrating newcomers (especially someone with another background and culture) into the creative team, first would offer the newcomer a marketing position in order that they may gain credibility and legitimacy.

Amongst the creative talents short-listed, Naomi Y., an American native with a passport from China, is one of the selected candidates the CEO wanted to work with.

After a short and bespoke induction program including meetings with some of the key people of the brand (Marketing, Communication, Retail Directors, workshops and factory visits) she accepts the deal.

3.3.2   Background and professional biography of the new Marketing/Creative

Naomi Y. has dual nationalities: US and Chinese.

She received a Bachelor of Arts in Economics and History from New York University and attended a summer program at the Saint Martin's School in London. She is totally fluent in English, Italian and Spanish and has an excellent command of French.

Her international career began in the fashion industry, with merchandising management roles in Japan and in Italy. Then was later given design responsibilities for American and Italian fashion brands in New York.

She has joined the Luxury Brand in 2004, as Marketing Development Director for Accessories.

3.3.3 A tough but valuable career path within the luxury brand

To start in a Marketing Development position was a tough experience for a creative but provided a distinct advantage for growing up within the brand:

1. Knowing the historical roots of the Luxury Brand's products portfolio.
2. Coping with the specific skills and savoir faire of the brand's Creative department.
3. Understanding the marketing function in the overall value chain: product brief, communication role, industrial and after sales issues, customer experience and data analysis, etc.

The departure of the CEO was an unexpected event to deal with. The challenge for her was to earn the confidence of the new CEO and his team.

Very pragmatic, the new CEO understood her strengths as being both in marketing and creation and recognized the added-value of her professional network with key actors of the Italian fashion industry. He promoted her to Designer in the leather goods division.

Two years later:

• She had built a true partnership with the CEO and gained his professional respect.
• She set-up an efficient design team, working with external designers, developers and factories in Italy.
• She had developed a collection that not only represented a significant percentage of leather goods profits, but also contributed to building up a consistent identity for leather goods.

3.3.4   Two lessons to learn: how to manage a creative career transition

Our long experience in seeking creative people for luxury brands, including those who come from international creative academies and those who are regularly in touch with the search market, show us that two factors are particularly important to master before joining a luxury brand:

Lesson 1: To succeed as a new creative in a luxury company one must **have strong specific personal traits** such as:

- **Tenacity** to overcome expected and unexpected events that may occur in the creative landscape.
- **Agility** to adapt to the overall culture, taking on board the brand's strategic orientation and appreciating the role of the founder/leader, the relationship style within the company and relationships with the key communication and marketing managers.
- **Ability to deal with ambiguity** especially when faced with people or organizational change.
- **Persuasion and influence skills** to assert one's vision of the world.
- **Innate curiosity** that leads to be open-minded to other cultures both professional and national.

Lesson 2: The CEO's ability and commitment to partner with a Creative

In our case study, the way the new CEO effectively led the creative in her role is a relevant example of what to do in this specific situation.

First of all, the CEO earns the respect of the individual by considering her expertise rather than her job title.

He then provides the room and resources for her creativity: A studio with the best and most up-to-date equipment; the opportunity to choose the internal resources she wants to work with.

Finally, the CEO senses her needs and keeps her motivated by preserving her from administrative and political distractions (he appointed a financial controller with a good understanding of creation issues). Day after day, he demonstrated to her that the company needed her talent and would help her succeed.

3.4   Case study 4: The Dior case, a successful leadership duo example

3.4.1   The situation of the Company early 2000

In the second half of the 90s, Dior was a brand that was in the middle of a complete reorganization: Its organization had previously lacked consistency (each divisional head seemed to have few constraints) and Bernard Arnault had hired John Galliano as Creative Director in 1996, wanting him to bring Dior back to the forefront of the luxury industry.

Sydney Toledano, who became president of Dior in March 1998, is the man that has achieved this.[3] One of his first moves was to reorganize the company with a single objective: make sure that John Galliano's creativity had an optimal impact on sales (see Figure 3.2).

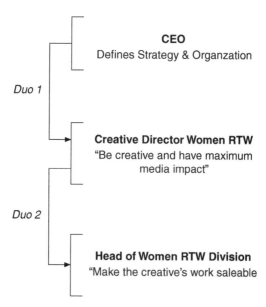

Figure 3.2   The new company organization

Dior's strategy was totally nonstandard and can best be characterized as eclectic. There were in fact not just one but three Creative Directors at Dior; John Galliano was Creative Director for women, Heidi Slimane for men and Victoire de Castellane for jewellery. Both Galliano and Slimane were given responsibilities for perfumes and cosmetics in 2001.[4]

The Creative Director is the person responsible for making sure that all elements of the company are consistent with the brand's vision. In 1996 John Galliano was transferred from Givenchy to Dior, in charge of women's wear design and image **(Duo 1 in the new company organization)**.

Valérie Hermann, the head of Dior women's RTW division since December 1998, **(Duo 2 in the new company organization)** and of the Galliano Company described Galliano as "more of a poet than a grocer".[5] She added "I am more of a grocer than a poet" providing us with a a classic example of the designer/businessperson duality in luxury. The fit that is evident between both of them, both at Dior and at John Galliano, is what lies behind the success of the brand. She herself speaks of "harmony."[6] John Galliano's profile nevertheless allowed him to understand the constraints of business. What she achieved, with strong support both from Sydney Toledano and his predecessor, François Beaufumé, is a magic blend of business and creation – that very blend that many brands only hope to achieve.

3.4.2   The Duo's achievements

They applied some basic business sense, apparel development and merchandising techniques:

- Sizes were standardized, based on the average French size of 38 models and not on the "super slim sample sizes of runway models."
- Selling results were fed back into the system to optimize new designs: *"We need more models in this material, bigger bags, less*

colors. The Logo collection for instance was a marketing idea. It works because the prices are right, but also because John has put all his creative twist in it," said Valérie Hermann.[7]

- The offer and price points was broadened.
- Deliveries were improved, increasing the number of pieces in the first shipments for pre-collection and main collection.
- The development team were able to focus on John Galliano's many creative ideas and transform them into salable items.
- One of Valérie Hermann's jobs was to scrutinize every Euro Galliano wanted to spend saying words like "be careful this model is too difficult to make, we will be way above acceptable prices."

3.4.3 The seven lessons to learn from this leadership duo

The Dior case shows that creation, business and organization can be optimized if the people fit well together. Beyond this case, we have observed other Leadership Duos as mentioned in Part 1.

All of them, act and behave together, as John Galliano and Valérie Hermann did in the Dior case, respecting critical and common factors, such as:

Lesson 1: Awareness of strengths and weaknesses
Duos realistically assess what they do well and where they need help.

Lesson 2: Complementary skills
Duos seek those who balance their own working styles and decision making approaches.

Lesson 3: Trust
Duos trust each other and are willing to put each other's needs ahead of their own.

Lesson 4: Raw intelligence
Duos bringinsightful observations and good judgment to the team's decision.

Lesson 5: Relevant knowledge
Duos bring experience that applies directly to the challenges they face.

Lesson 6: Strong communication channels
Duos speak to each other frequently and directly. They often work in the same or adjacent spaces.

Lesson 7: Motivation
Duos are highly committed to the success of the business and each other.

Guccio Gucci and his son Rodolfo, Florence Gucci store, late 1940s (Courtesy of Gucci)

A luxury talent methodology

Introduction

The generation that drove the successes at Cartier, Louis Vuitton, Hermès, Swatch, Armani and other famous iconic luxury brands has retired or is close to retirement (see Figure 4.1) and the industry will need to find new talent to replace them (see press releases on pages 134 & 135).

Considering the characteristics of luxury's Top 100 board members (see Part 2) and our analysis of luxury leadership competencies (see below), the luxury industry must find leaders that:

• Present a balanced leadership profile that blends intelligence with relevant competencies (creative, intuitive, rational and social) in order to be efficient;
• Have operated in different key geographic regions, such as Asia or America, to understand the different cultural characteristics both of employees and of customers;
• Switch easily between different time frames, from long-term thinking to short-term operating;
• Bring change management skills to an organization in order to reinvent the business model, while preserving the "mystery" of a brand's DNA;
• Have great attention to retail and customer issues, acknowledging the central role of sales staff;

- Have the talent to represent a brand as its ambassador and a great cultural ability to interact well with a very demanding international clientele;
- Develop specific leadership skills to work efficiently with creatives and designers;
- Fit in with the founder's vision of the world and those of the family members who are inevitably involved in the business;
- Understand the characteristics of the brand's organizational culture;
- Possess the cultural background (from their family values and their education) that allows them to master the intricacies of a very "cultural" business.

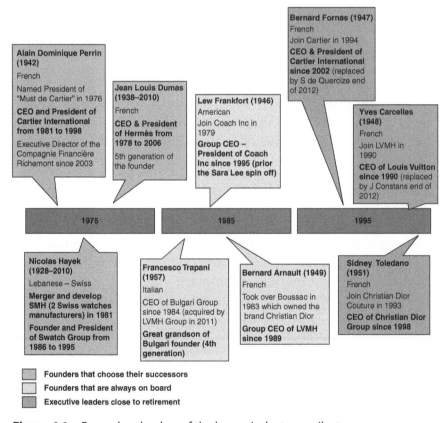

Figure 4.1 Exemplary leaders of the luxury industry – milestones

To achieve this, luxury brands need to address this issue with a new mindset. First of all, they need to consider succession planning as a proactive and continuous process rather than the result of a traditional and reactive "rat race." The second key point is to have a clear and shared view about the competencies needed to face these challenges. Specific tools should be used such as regular "talent risk analysis." It is also important to look at leaders or key people with rare competencies that are nearing retirement in order to identify critical roles and leadership skills required for business success.

With this new approach the luxury industry could retain those of the current talent pool who grew up close to the previous entrepreneurial generation while attracting and developing new leader profiles from both inside and outside the industry capable of bringing a fresh perspective while being able to cope with luxury's critical cultural nuances.

Part 4 is the academic part of this book: It presents a methodology for tackling the luxury leadership challenges mentioned above. It provides innovative conceptual models and tools which will be illustrated throughout by using case studies and tangible examples based on real situations.

- Section **"The Luxury Competencies Model"** provides a framework designed to identify and replicate talent.
- Section **"Developing customer service"** illustrates the way to develop customer services with a significant focus on the retail staff, including a talent diagnosis and critical things to know about recruiting and rewarding them.
- Section **"Cultivating creative/designer talent"** provides key insights about Creatives and Designers with some clues to understand these very particular people, including practical tools to recruit and lead them accordingly.
- Section **"Addressing the digital age"** gives our view as to how the digital age – a major challenge for the luxury industry – should be addressed.

Insight: Luxury industry trend/moves and profiles

Press release – September 2011

"Yves Carcelle, chief executive of Louis Vuitton, will stand aside at the end of the next year to be replaced by Jordi Constans, a senior executive of Danone, the French yoghurt group.

The move, announced by Louis Vuitton's parent company LVMH on Wednesday, reflects a trend among luxury goods groups to hire senior executives from the consumer goods industry as their rapid expansion into emerging markets mirrors that of Danone, Unilever or Procter & Gamble two decades ago.

It also brings to a close one of the longest and most successful careers in fashion. Mr Carcelle, who has led LVMH since 1990, is credited with having made Louis Vuitton one of the most profitable and ubiquitous luxury goods brands.

Mr Constans, 47, who is Spanish, most recently was the executive vice-president of fresh dairy products at Danone. He will shadow Mr Carcelle throughout 2012 before taking over the job of chief executive, LVMH said.

Mr Arnault said: "I am delighted that Jordi Constans is joining the group. Initially, he will have the privilege of working with Yves Carcelle, who has led Louis Vuitton with remarkable success since 1990."

Press release – March 2012

"Swiss luxury goods group Richemont said on Monday it has appointed Stanislas de Quercize to take over from Bernard Fornas as chief executive of top-of-the-range jewellery and watch maker Cartier.

De Quercize, current CEO of Richemont subsidiary Van Cleef & Arpels, will replace Fornas at the end of the year, when he is due to retire, Richemont said.

$\rightarrow$

Cartier, which is expanding rapidly in emerging markets such as Brazil and China, is the largest of Richemont's luxury brands, which also include Vacheron Constantin, IWC and Montblanc.

"Losing someone of Fornas' stature is going to be difficult – he did much to build Cartier's momentum over the last decade, improving profitability and growth," said Kepler analyst Jon Cox, who noted that Cartier represents half of group sales and two-thirds of operating profit.

But Cox also said De Quercize had turned Van Cleef & Arpels around since his appointment, making the brand profitable and growing its credibility with buyers of high-end jewellery.

"He has been with the group a long time, knows Cartier from his time there – so the brand looks to be in good hands."

4.1   The Luxury Competencies Model: A framework to identify and replicate talent

At this stage, managing luxury executives means asking critical questions that will help define tomorrow's luxury leaders:

1. What competencies differentiate luxury professionals working in high performing luxury brands from those working outside the luxury industry?
2. Are these competencies specific to the luxury industry? And are they adapted to tackle upcoming luxury business challenges and issues?
3. Do all luxury leaders have the same leadership profile?
4. Are luxury leaders "transferable" to other industries?
5. Are these specific competencies taught and developed in existing Business Schools or International Creative Schools ?

To answer these questions we suggest the use of a framework introduced by Marie Laure Djelic and Michel Gutsatz[1] that presents a competency-based approach for the luxury goods industry.

The **Luxury Competencies Model** (LCM) is a comprehensive and tangible set of clear and critical behaviors that a luxury executive *employs* in a real situation. This framework demonstrates that luxury leaders do have specific competencies.

Thanks to the LCM we will develop additional aspects regarding the profile of tomorrows' luxury leaders such as luxury relevant knowledge, luxury leadership styles and specific transferable "savoir-faire" or know-how.

Likewise, and in order to be concrete, we have designed two LCM case studies showing on one hand how to evaluate an executive board's key competencies and on the other hand the decision process which should be mastered in a C-level recruitment. These two case studies will demonstrate how to operate with the LCM.

4.1.1   The Luxury Competencies Model: description

Over the past 10 years, the authors have counselled various key players in the luxury industry on a wide range of topics, such as executive search and assessment assignments, executive education, luxury conferences and surveys.

As a result, we have been able to conceive a strong and pertinent Luxury Competencies Model (see Figure 4.2). Its aim is to specify the competencies needed by luxury executives to deliver value for luxury brands.

The Luxury Competencies Model is based on:

- **Four key managerial capabilities**
- **Five luxury leadership styles**
- **Two unique factors developed in Part 1**

Four key managerial capabilities[2]

Key Managerial Capability 1: Luxury relevant knowledge is a fundamental basic that a leader must acquire and master to act

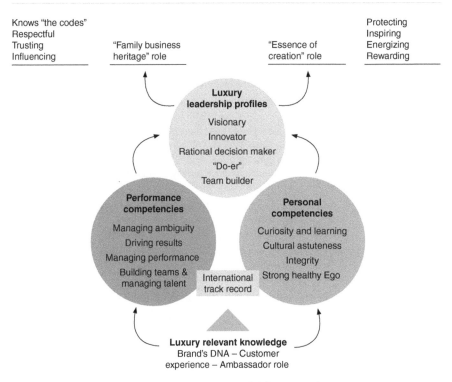

Knows "the codes"
Respectful
Trusting
Influencing

"Family business heritage" role

"Essence of creation" role

Protecting
Inspiring
Energizing
Rewarding

Luxury leadership profiles

Visionary
Innovator
Rational decision maker
"Do-er"
Team builder

Performance competencies

Managing ambiguity
Driving results
Managing performance
Building teams & managing talent

International track record

Personal competencies

Curiosity and learning
Cultural astuteness
Integrity
Strong healthy Ego

Luxury relevant knowledge
Brand's DNA – Customer experience – Ambassador role

Figure 4.2 The Luxury Competencies Model framework

efficiently in this particular landscape. The Brand's DNA, the ability to get things done, an intimate knowledge of the customer experience and role as the brand ambassador are examples of industry relevant knowledge.

Key Managerial Capability 2: International Track Record. This is critical for performing in the luxury industry, which is both an international and a cultural business.

We can break this down into three major domains: *business acumen, impact and impression, and communication.* Figure 4.3 provides a detailed description of each.

A track record of outstanding accomplishments in relevant business situations such as developing brand awareness, designing a new collection that pays off and dealing with a profitable selective distribution network are all valuable.

Luxury business acumen	> Has deep and broad understanding of the customer and luxury landscape
	> Quickly grasps key trends and business drivers
	> Has a good understanding and knowledge of the core disciplines: the craftsmanship's experience and the retail experience
	> Knows how to network and connect with the luxury and business community
	> Knows the brand's key business competitors and their specificities: main actors, sales experts, creations and collections
	> Keeps up to date with high jewelry and watch markets and sales: recent deals, auction house activity, client expectations
Impact & impression	> Is aware of the impression he/she makes and he/she masters the "art of execution"
	> Is an attentive, empathetic and responsive listener
	> Has a smooth, enticing and elegant style and treats people at all levels with respect
Communication	> Communicates passion, energy, intensity, and excitement
	> Uses examples and stories that engender a pleasure of buying for the client
	> Is able to adapt his/her message and manner to people who are different from him/herself

Figure 4.3   Luxury relevant knowledge

Gaining these business achievements in luxury's key geographic regions (e.g. The Asian or American markets for a European native; Asian or EMEA markets for an American native) demonstrates an ability to:

- Deal with the stress, frustration and confusion of an international work
- Develop transnational social skills an cross cultural sensitivity
- Think away from stereotypes and develop effective thinking and to be open-minded about the cultural differences of employees and customers.

Key Managerial Capability 3: Performance Competencies are those that are critical to creating value, to attracting and managing diverse key talents – from Creatives to a "Grand Vendeur" – and to delivering results accordingly.

Figure 4.4 details four major performance competencies which are essential for luxury: *managing ambiguity, driving results, managing performance and team building and managing talent.*

Managing ambiguity	> Sets a clear direction for others in times of uncertainty and change > Follows business instincts in situations where there is certainty of outcome
Driving results	> Proactively manages the client focus; demonstrates a sense of creativity to sustain client relationship > Has successfully managed significant deals quarter after quarter over many years and acquired new clients for the brand > Has a proven track record in making deals that balance a variety of factors (e.g. costs, risk, short-term versus long-term, brand policy) to achieve an optimal outcome for the brand/the organization
Managing performance	> Translates over-arching business goals into specific objectives for each member of the team > Holds people accountable for agreed-to results > Identifies and keeps others focused on the most important metrics that drive the business
Team building & managing talent	> Forges strong diverse teams of people with multiple perspectives and talent > Delegates significant responsibility to team members and holds them accountable > Gets personally and actively involved in sourcing, selecting, developing and retaining top talent for key positions

Figure 4.4 Performance competencies

Key Managerial Capability 4: Personal competencies. They are the broad spectrum of personal and cultural attributes that leaders have acquired through the course of their personal and professional development. This includes the personality traits taken from his/her own cultural background, family background, early education and early international exposure, further education, initial professional background and professional development in an organization.

Within the luxury landscape, these personal traits are critical in helping the aspiring leader learn and effectively deal with international clients, acting at ease in the locations where their high-net worth clientele "play and spend" all over the world.

Figure 4.5 details five major Personal Competencies that are essential in luxury: *Analytical skills, Curiosity and cultural background, Learning agility, Integrity, and Strong, healthy ego.*

Analytical skills	> Is able to dig deep into the details of the business while staying focused on the big picture > Uses information collected efficiently to pepare sales > Has a global mindset: thinks across disciplines, industries, cultures, scenarios, etc.
Curiosity & cultural background	> Has a deep interest in a wide range of client interests: art and culture, literature, world news and business, social and charity events, etc. > Has knowledge of the far reaches of the luxury core discipline > Persistently questions until he/she has ascertained the client's need
Learning agility	> Absorbs new facts, data and information rapidly > Has the capacity to be open; to explore areas where there are no right answers > Is humble and patient enough to ask questions to ensure he/she understands the situation
Integrity	> Respects the brand's core values and principles when with clients > Maintains well-articulated core values and expected behavior, and hold others to the same standard with no exceptions > Follows through on commitments despite difficulties or complications. Is totally available for the client
Strong, healthy Ego	> Has the confidence to deal with both the Family and "high ticket sales" > Admits failures and major mistakes readily and identifies lessons gained fom them > Is resilient in the face of failure; handles setbacks without losing confidence or drive

Figure 4.5   Personal competencies

The Five luxury leadership styles

The Luxury Leadership Styles define the dominant way leaders deal with both people and situations in an organizational context. They are based on personal behavioral competencies and "underlying" characteristics that are linked to personal traits and motives, social roles and constructed self-image. The importance of behavioral competencies lies in the fact that they can not only have an impact on performance in a given job but also on the development of the entire professional life of an individual. What is significant is the identification of sets of behavioral competencies found systematically together.

Five predominant sets of behavioral competencies have been identified,[3] which we named "Luxury Leadership Styles": *Visionary, Innovator, Team builder, Do-er and Rational Decision Maker* (see Figure 4.6).

Figure 4.6 The five luxury leadership styles

Each of the five dominant Leadership Styles will be described within the following framework:

- Examples of a management attributes which a person with a given Luxury Leadership Style is good at.
- **Key dominant behaviors** that illustrate the Luxury Leadership Style.
- Relevant business situations in which the Leadership Luxury Style is most effective and **works best**.

Leadership Style 1: The Visionary Leader or "strategist"
The Visionary **is good at**: providing a holistic vision, developing strategic direction, thinking out-of-the-box to create new organizational ways of working and partnering, and generating future goals for the business.

The Visionary **dominant behaviors** are:

- Excellent at abstract, imaginative thinking and aesthetic sensitivity
- Ability to see the big picture and to plan accordingly
- Possession of a spiral sense of time, where time moves forward but also comes back to include the past
- Excellent at aligning vision with strategy
- Sensitivity to weak signals and nuances which may later develop into trends

The Visionary leadership style **works best when**: times are turbulent or uncertain, and changes in the environment require new directions.

Leadership Style 2: The Innovator Leader or "idea generator"
The Innovator **is good at**: focusing on the new. He has a great capacity to solve extremely difficult problems, breaking the rules when necessary.

The Innovator's **dominant behaviors** are:

- Great drive to pursue his/her ideas
- Creative and imaginative with capacity to take risks
- Always on the lookout for future possibilities: new projects, new activities, new procedures
- Will stretch themselves to achieve any goal

The Innovator leadership style **works best when**: generating new ideas and ways of doing things within an organization.

Leadership Style 3: The Team Builder Leader or "coach"
The Team Builder **is good at**: creating high performance teams with different cultural backgrounds.

The Team Builder's **dominant behaviors** are:

- Inspiring trust thanks to his/her affinity for people and cooperation

- Talent for handling difficult interpersonal and group situations
- Capacity for forging diverse teams of people with multiple talent
- Excellence at listening and responding

The Team Builder leadership style **works best when**: networking with people and using them to accomplish objectives.

Leadership Style 4: The Do-er Leader or "change catalyst"
The Do-er **is good at**: mastering and creating new organizational "blueprints" with a very "can do" attitude.

The Do-er's **dominant behaviors** are:

- Great capacity for identifying and selling the need for change
- Creative when turning abstract concepts into practical action
- Ability to align vision, strategy and behavior
- Very talented at monitoring performance and at leading people
- Gets very involved in projects
- Leads by example

The Do-er leadership style **works best when**: situations of great transformation after a merger or acquisition, a turnaround project, delivering a culture change project.

Leadership Style 5: The Rational Decision Maker Leader or "efficient"
The Rational Decision Maker **is good at**: setting up the structures and systems needed to support an organization's objectives.

The Rational Decision Maker's **dominant behaviors** are:

- Good at implementing process-based actions
- Great self-discipline, very reliable efficient and conscientious
- Has a directive style of leadership
- Excellent at time management, remaining cool headed in situations of stress
- Uses conceptual thinking and very analytical vision of situations

The Rational Decision Maker leadership style **works best when**: creating order out of chaos.

These five luxury leadership styles are interconnected:

1. The Visionary and the Rational Decision Maker appear to be very different from each other, with taking a holistic view of situations and the other a more analytical one. Without a doubt, these two leadership styles correspond to very different people, but they have a common characteristic: they are both always associated with the Innovator leadership style. This means that innovation could be led by persons with two very different leadership styles.
2. A Visionary is often (but not always) at the same time a Do-er.
3. Although the Team Builder is clearly a separate leadership style, it can also be found associated either with the Visionary or with the Rational Decision Maker.

This leads to a tentative map of the profiles, which can be said to characterize leaders of the luxury industry (see Figure 4.7).

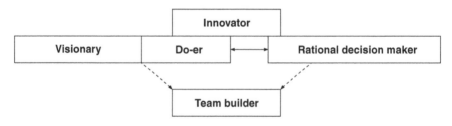

Figure 4.7 How the five profiles are linked

Two unique factors developed in Part 1

One must also consider that to become a luxury leader the most sought-after profiles are those that can successfully manage the two unique factors of the luxury industry that we identified in Part 1:

• The Family Business Heritage: knowing the family codes, respecting them, being trusted by the family members and using influencing skills when necessary.

- The Essence of Creation: to be mastered (or acquired) in order to protect them from daily organizational issues, to encourage creative inspiration and work, energizing the creatives and reward them specifically and accordingly.

4.1.2   Applying the Luxury Competencies Model: case studies

The following two case studies, adapted from "real situations," will illustrate the way to use practically the Luxury Competencies Model as a management tool.

Case study 1: Recruiting a General Manager for a Swiss family business

The brief in short

The company: A 50-year-old Swiss family watch brand is seeking a General Manager to leverage the company's expansion and awareness for the both America and Asia markets

The mission: In-line with the family business strategy:

- **Lead the development and profitability of the watch activity.**
- **Develop new products in close cooperation with the creative vision and the help of about 80 people including marketers, designers and trades people.**

The expected candidate: A team builder who understands product development and is highly growth oriented.

Status: Executive reporting to the President (second generation), owner and CEO of the company.

An international head hunter firm has been requested to manage the search through its international offices.

→

The external selected candidate's profiles

Candidate 1: Paul F, 38 years old – French citizen. French Business Diploma.

He joined an independent watch-making family business ten years ago, where he started as product manager and grew to the Marketing Development Director role. For the last two years he has led the US market as Country Regional Manager.

Candidate 2: John W K, 45 years old – dual Swiss and German nationalities – Engineering diploma + MBA (US Business School).

He began his professional career with a Swiss watch manufacturer, first as a development engineer, then as the Industrial Director (15 years) before joining the HQ of a Luxury Group He is currently COO of an Italian Luxury Group.

Candidate 3: Michael O, 42 years old – UK citizen – Cambridge University diploma.

Spent ten years as a "right hand" to a Swiss family luxury business, in the position of GM.

For the past year, he has led the family brand's integration in a French Luxury Group as a Vice President of the business operation.

Analysis and comments

All the three candidates have gained professional experience within a luxury brand, so in this case we need to evaluate:

1. The candidates' leadership capacity and ability to cope with the organizational culture and values of the family brand in the long term. In other words, will they fit well with:
   • The family's sensibilities: e.g. partnering with the CEO & President's business vision;
   • The Brand's DNA: the watch-making savoir faire;

$\rightarrow$

- The capacity to lead a team of diverse talents (marketers, watchmakers, engineers, etc.) in a very specific environment which requires subtle management skills.

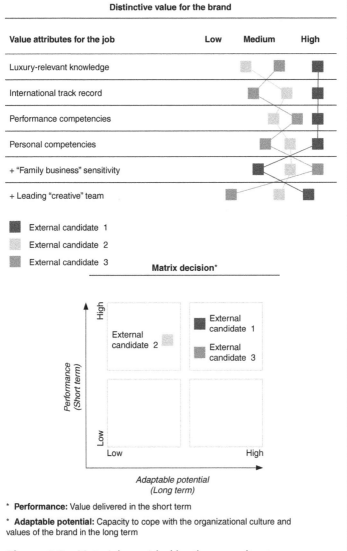

Figure 4.8 Material provided by the consultant

2. Their ability to contribute value in the short term:
   - To function daily with the emotionally charged family members that are involved in the company's development;
   - To manage the development of successful new products;

Considering the case elements, **Candidate 1** seems to have relevant experience and skills that could match. Therefore, his background with a family business provides him with a distinct advantage which, as a first step, get him a meeting with the CEO & President.

Case study 2: Assessing the leadership style of a luxury executive board

The brief in short

The company: A US family luxury brand with a wide product portfolio including clothes, leather goods and accessories

Key elements:

- 1000 people worldwide; two factories (of which one is outsourced in Morocco) and two workshops for special orders maintained and controlled in the United States;
- 10 own retail flagships in the top luxury cities and a strong worldwide wholesale network (30 external retail, 150 corners, etc.);
- Two historic creatives (responsible for clothes and leather) and an international pool of designers which are used depending on the collection.

Business challenges:

- Pursue a growth strategy despite the economic downturn; acquire a European partner to help address this particular market.

$\rightarrow$

- Gain clear knowledge of both its capabilities and changes in the luxury landscape.
- Develop internal talent to fill creative mission-critical roles accordingly.

Ownership: the family – the founder and his two sons – owns the majority of shares.

The executive board profile

CEO profile: 55 years old, Italian, became the CEO of the company thanks to his role as lawyer to the founder eight years ago. Born in an industrial family in Milan, he received his law diploma from a UK Business School and built, through his role as CEO, an outstanding international network in the luxury business community.

Finance Director profile: 43 years old, US citizen – MBA (US Business School), son of the founder. He started his career in IT (blue chip company) before moving to consumer goods where he took on finance responsibilities for a fragrance brand. He has been in the finance role for the last two years.

Marketing and Sales Director profile: 38 years old, French and US citizens – Diploma in Literature (La Sorbonne). She began her career for a French jeweler as Distribution Manager before joining its US subsidiary as a Retail Manager. A fast tracker, she was hired to develop the brand's awareness through retail and selective distribution expansion in the European and BRIC markets.

Operations Director profile: 48 years old, dual US and Greek nationalities – Engineering Diploma and an Executive Business graduate program (AMP – Swiss Business School). He started his career with an international consulting firm where he was responsible for supply-chain issues for a wide range of industries. Joined the company three years ago, after an internal assignment, to lead global operations: factory production, supply chain management and after-sales service, from the United States.

→

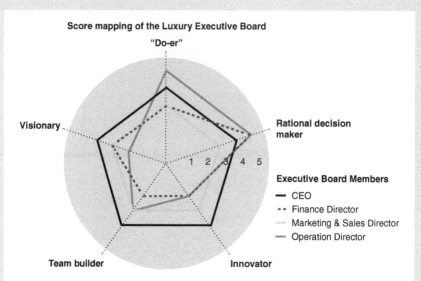

Figure 4.9   Input provided by the consultant regarding leadership styles

The family members ask an international consulting firm, expert in Human Due Diligence, to lead an executive board audit in order to assess the capability of the board to deal with the business challenges in the coming year.

The consultant's suggestion

Usually, a Human Due Diligence report (HDD) reveals the key audit findings about the strengths, the weaknesses and the future focus for the company, with some recommendations for particular actions to develop individuals, the organization and the family's business governance.

In this case, the leadership issue is a key point regarding the business challenges that the Executive Board has to face. The HDD report could suggest recommendations such as the following:

- A coaching program to help key managers acquire experience and skills that will enable them to adapt and fit with new organization in the event of a merger.

$\rightarrow$

- Identify probable risks and challenging situations and provide an action plan to tackle those with the highest potential.
- Custom design a seminar in cooperation with a business school with a Family Business program in order to challenge the company's mindset.
- Lead a team building initiative to reveal the governance leadership dominant style, etc.

4.1.3   Two important questions

In Part 3, we highlighted how an executive leader coming from outside the luxury industry succeeded by achieving exceptional results (see the Robert Polet case study). In the present section, we want to tackle the two following questions:

- **Are management talents that come from within the luxury industry "portable" outside? Which luxury specific skills and know-hows could be mapped onto another industry?**
- **Given the importance of the organizational culture of each luxury brand, specific development programs can only be developed in-house. Should these luxury specific competencies be developed in in-house Academies?**

Insight 1: Are luxury leaders portable?

Portability is based on two criteria: 1) understanding whether luxury executives will have the skills required to fit into another industry 2) is their know-how transferable to another business. Positively combining these two criteria will maximize the chance of successfully integrating an executive coming from the luxury industry.

- Figure 4.10 (luxury leadership portability) defines key criteria to determine whether a luxury leader's abilities will match another industry (see Figure 4.9). It provides some first clues

$\rightarrow$

to illustrate: four types of human skills: strategic, company specific, industry and relationships – that we have listed from most portable to least and their related luxury-specific know-how or savoir faire.

- As a result, luxury leaders that have developed abilities, such as very strong consumer awareness, the highest standards of creativity, spirit of excellence, the art of selling "design" internally and the capacity to lead diverse team of multiple talent, are definitely portable. For each of these abilities we have described the situation in which a transfer could be effective.

Skill type	Luxury-specific "know how"	Transferable when ...
Strategic human capital: expertise in cyclical markets, growth	*Very strong awareness among consumers, worldwide presence, retail and wholesale distribution management*	*The industry's strategic needs match the new executive skills*
Company-specific human capital: knowledge about routines and procedures, corporate culture and informal management systems	*Specific time frame, spirit of excellence, exceptional art of living*	*Many similarities exist between the systems and culture of the executive's former industry and those of your industry*
Industry human capital: technical, customer or supplier knowledge unique to the industry	*Very strong awareness of consumers, highest standard of creativity, spirit of excellence, exceptional art of selling 'design' internally*	*The industry's needs strategic design skills and familiarity with luxury customers*
Relationship human capital: creation and productivity derived from participation in teams	*Capacity to lead diverse teams of different talents: designer, sales, marketers as well as manufacturing forces*	*The industry needs a new executive to provide "organized space" and resources for their creative activity*

(right margin: ▲ Rarely transferable ... ▼ Often transferable)

Figure 4.10   Luxury leader abilities that will match another industry

Source: Adapted from B. Groysberg, A. Mc Lean and N. Noria (2007): "Are leaders portable," *Harvard Business Review*.

At this stage we do not have many concrete examples of great luxury leaders who moved successfully to another industry, but that will certainly change soon.

Despite the fact that the luxury industry is a very attractive, comfortable and valuable place to work and build an international career path, we believe that future challenges and changes will accelerate moves from this industry to others, such as *Fast-Moving Consumer Goods, Private Banking, Leisure and Hospitality, and Automotive.*

In these industries, dealing with the upper segment of clientele, inspiring notions of craftsmanship, savoir faire and experience, managing teams of multiple and diverse talent such as the Creative, Designer and digital profiles are critical in these industries, which is why executive talent from the luxury industry would be valuable to them.

Insight 2: Why should luxury specific competencies be developed in in-house Academies?

Many companies have started devising their own in-house University (or Academy) system, appreciating that talent sourcing is a major issue for the luxury industry. The issue here is both quantitative and qualitative: will a new Executive (or Sales Assistant or Designer) fit into the brand's organizational culture? Managers need an accurate understanding of the brand's culture to find their way inside the company and to act effectively. Luxury-specific competencies can be taught or learnt from experience but an efficient manager/executive can fail when moved from one brand to another (even within the same group). This is mainly due to a lack of understanding of the brand's organizational culture (See our case study in Part 3 – a difficult succession plan in a family luxury business).

The primary objective of an in-house Academy is to impart a common organizational culture. Two exemplary actors of the luxury industry have been instrumental in designing such Academies and in understanding the importance of the organizational culture: Concetta Lanciaux, former Executive VP of Human Resources at LVMH, and Franco Cologni, who has had an impressive career with Cartier and Richemont Group.

$\rightarrow$

The Concetta Lanciaux Heritage

"If the luxury industry has real icons she is one of the greatest innovators; the person most responsible for raising the quality of training and people-development in the global luxury industry" in the words of Michael Pedraza, CEO of the research think tank Luxury Institute.

As a Bernard Arnault "right hand woman" – successively as HR Group Chairman, then Executive VP of Synergies, and as Advisor to the President – she helped him build his LVMH business into the world's most prestigious powerhouse, finding synergies across the organization as well as taking care of more the 40 companies including their presidents and chief executives.

The big challenge was to understand all the brands and help find the best designers for them in close collaboration with Bernard Arnault. Likewise, coming from Carnegie Mellon and Intel (which was the state-of-the-art in management), she had to manage the paradox of talent mobility versus brand creativity. When she began, most firms were small, family-owned companies without graduates or succession planning.

Thanks to her leadership, LVMH:

1. Hired staff with experience in other industries such as consumer goods and selected people with "good taste" and the ability to cope with both creative people and family business heritage.
2. Partnered with French Business School ESSEC to launch the LVMH Chair.
3. Carried-out numerous original initiatives for young people in France and abroad that provide high school students, art students, young artists and designers as well as those closer to the group with new work opportunities.
4. Instituted strong companywide induction program and training programs as well as on-the-job training to introduce the world of luxury to novices to the industry. The principal goal

$\rightarrow$

is to educate and awake the LVMH "newcomers" on the know-how, skills, spirit of excellence, the ethics that each luxury brand conveys through its products.

5. Developed the concept of LVMH House – located in London – where global company presidents, members of management committees and heads of subsidiaries can share their knowledge and experience, to develop a common vision of LVMH as a learning organization capable of developing and retaining human capital and enhance synergies through cross fertilization between all companies and functions within the group.

6. Promoted the Human Resources function and appointed competent HR Directors as executive committee members within each luxury brand to address talent management challenges.

The Creative Academy: An idea from Franco Cologni

Franco Cologni's career in top management has always been accompanied by a passion for the arts and crafts as an opinion leader, journalist, writer and publisher. He was the brain behind numerous key international projects. The Creative Academy project is one such project which he suggested and delivered to the Richemont Group.

The Creative Academy is an international postgraduate school of design, based in Milan, which gives specialized training in design for applied arts, in particular in jewellery, watch-making and fashion accessories. The Creative Academy's mission is to offer young professionals of the future the tools necessary to meet the constantly evolving demands of production world.

The young talents at The Academy have the opportunity to learn about the fascinating world of the luxury good design from a privileged perspective and, with the support of design experts and teachers, can conceive projects for some of the most prestigious brands in the luxury industry.

→

Regarding his idea to create a design school, Cologni is quoted as saying:[4]

"The conviction that discovering new design artists, cultivating them, educating them and, if possible, keeping them for one's own is the most profitable form of investment for the luxury goods world."

"This led to the idea for an innovative project like the one I suggested to the Richemont Group which has welcomed the important opportunity of being directly involved in training."

"Today, Creative Academy produces highly specialised young creative artists, for the Richemont Group and the luxury goods sector in general, through a direct passage from school to the workplace."

4.1.4   Conclusion: principles for luxury training

These two valuable examples from the industry's leading luxury groups provide us with some important principles to bear in mind when addressing the way to better train the specific luxury competencies:

1. The objective of an in-house academy is to provide specific training for each brand and general edification for the group's organizational culture.
2. An in-house training program should not be replicable outside the group.
3. Creation and design are core elements of a brand's identity: training programs should be built around them. In a sense the an in-house training school will be a "mirror" of the Atelier or factory.
4. The in-house training school philosophy should be based on the apprenticeship model, valuing the transmission of knowledge between master and apprentice or mentor and mentee.

5. Because of the international dimension of a luxury brand and the very different cultural attitudes to luxury and service, the in-house training school should be adapted to all major cultures.

6. Having the CEO, Artistic Director and other leaders of the brand directly involved in the teaching program will allow students to learn from those who deal every day in the work world.

Based on these above principles, we suggest designing a framework for a Luxury Talent House, a place to both learn and share the luxury experience (see Figure 4.11). The key elements are:

Top Faculty Pool: all of them come from well-known and well-regarded business schools and/or design schools. They possess academic expertise in strategy, marketing/sales, digital, and change management and teach appropriate business cases relevant to the luxury industry issues

Top Luxury Professional Pool: they act for well-known luxury brands in CEO, Artistic or Retail Management positions and are

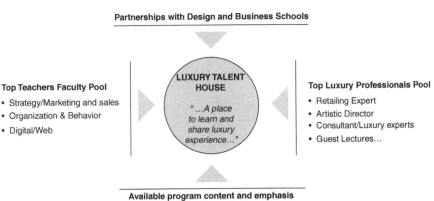

Partnerships with Design and Business Schools

Top Teachers Faculty Pool
- Strategy/Marketing and sales
- Organization & Behavior
- Digital/Web

LUXURY TALENT HOUSE
" ...A place to learn and share luxury experience..."

Top Luxury Professionals Pool
- Retailing Expert
- Artistic Director
- Consultant/Luxury experts
- Guest Lectures...

Available program content and emphasis
- Specifc analysis of the different luxury sectors
- Managing creative process
- Cultural trends and major aesthetic avenues
- Customer experience
- Digital issues: social media, e-reputation
- French/Italian language and culture...

Figure 4.11   The Luxury Talent House framework

passionate about communicating and explaining their luxury experience

A Brand Philosophy: the way the brand wishes to organize its academy so as to embed it into its organizational culture

It can, for instance, be built with an emphasis on transmission (for crafts-oriented brands) or on storytelling (for brands with strong heritage)

Examples of possible program contents:

- Understanding the Luxury Business Characteristics
- Managing the Creative Process
- Consumer Experience
- Digital Issues: Social Media, e-reputation
- Cultural Trends and Aesthetics Avenues
- French and Italian Language and Culture

4.2 Developing customer service

Introduction

Retail is now a top priority for many luxury brands. Why? Because in the luxury industry, which is built around creation, customers come second – therefore, a customer-experience culture is not central to the industry. In a sense, even retail is a newly acquired skill: the product, store concept and visual merchandising have always been more important than the sales experience itself.

The new challenge luxury brands face is to improve customer loyalty which can only be done at the store level, by developing service and customer relationships. In other words, luxury brands must become luxury *service* companies. Three objectives are critical here:

- **Develop clienteling:** Each client must be recognized as such and all his/her personal information treasured. Clienteling means establishing a personal relationship between a salesperson and a client. This is achieved through specific attitudes and with the support of technology (database management).

- **Make service the cornerstone of client relationship:** Shopping by appointment, the availability of a personal sales shopper, delivering purchases, sending handwritten thank you notes; these are just a few examples of the services a client should get in a luxury store. Luxury brands have to work on the recognition of customer journeys – and think of their stores as being a critical part of a journey that often begins on the web.
- **Recognize the central role of the sales staff:** Salespeople have an essential role to play in identifying the client, in caring for his/her wants and in delivering the very best service. Retail career tracks have to be nurtured, innovative compensation systems built (mixing fixed salaries, individual variable and collective variable parts), specific on-the-job training programs created.

Innovation in luxury marketing development means meeting new needs, introducing new entry-point lines rather than reducing prices, providing a truly exceptional level of service, promoting and selling luxury products using alternative distribution channels including e-commerce, co-creating products with the help of customers and handling the young consumers that already seem to be poised to purchase expensive luxury products online. This has a major consequence: marketing competencies are changing. Luxury marketers will be key players in building this new customer experience. They have to master both distribution and communication channels, because the boundaries are blurring: internet, mobile phones and the stores are places where the brand both sells and communicates, holding a conversation with its customers.

A relevant example of these transformations is the recent acquisition by Richemont of the successful online fashion store Net-A-Porter: its unique expertise in e-commerce and in building customer loyalty is critical to the luxury industry.

Luxury brands that put the right talent in place to rethink their retail and service operations while upgrading their marketing approach to better understand and serve the customer, will gain a tangible competitive advantage.

Sales staff is a key population in the luxury industry and must be addressed with a better care. To succeed in the future, luxury brands must put sales management on the level as design, product marketing or communication strategy.

This major challenge can be addressed by using some of the concrete and comprehensive elements of the toolbox designed for the book, "Luxury Retail Management"[5] and through a number of new retail concept approaches.

4.2.1   Retail talent diagnosis

A "Retail talent diagnosis" will outline the key points to keep in mind regarding retail's omni-channel challenges: new way of thinking, the war for retail talent, organization standards and new retail profiles.

The retail toolbox will be used to illustrate how to provide excellence in service and set up and develop an appropriate HR retail policy with particular attention to:

• The "behavioral approach" to recruiting retail candidates
• Clear and relevant career retail opportunities
• A fair reward system including compensation and benefits

The following sections will provide a better understanding of those retail challenges and some appropriate insights to help address them.

Step 1 – Thinking retail

What attributes and behaviors have changed and how, regarding talent mindset, employee value proposition, leaders development and the question of customer experience (see Figure 4.12)

	The Old Way	The New Way
Retail talent mindset	Store Director is responsible for retail management	All managers – starting with the CEO – are accountable for strengthening their retail talent pool
Employee Value Proposition (EVP)	We provide career perspective within the brand	We shape our brand, even our strategy, to attract talented people in our retail organization
Recruiting	Recruiting is like purchasing	Recruiting is like marketing
Developing leaders	We think development happens in training programs	We fuel development through stretch jobs, coaching and mentoring
Customer experience	We focus on clientele that is "worth it"	We offer each segment of our clientele an appropriate service level to nurture those relationships

Figure 4.12 New ways of thinking of retail talent

Step 2 – The priorities

The critical questions that brands must ask themselves in order to prepare for the war for retail talent are as follows:

1. Is retail one of your top three priorities?
2. Are you spending a significant part of your time strengthening your retail talent pool? Have you made retail talent your job?
3. Are you and all your key people explicitly held accountable for strengthening your retail talent pool?
4. Do you have a winning EVP (employee value proposition) that attracts talented people to your retail organization?
5. Do you know the attrition rate of your high-performing sales people and why they are leaving? Do you have initiatives in place to reduce these regretted losses?
6. Does your brand have a written recruiting strategy, similar in rigor to your marketing strategies?

7. Do you regularly shower your top retail performers with development job opportunities, significantly differentiated compensation, and real mentoring?

Step 3 – The organization

What is your retail organization structure?

All companies and brands will have their own specific organization structure which will often depend on the size of their operations. As soon as a significant number of stores needs to be managed in a given region, at least three levels of responsibilities need to be organized:

- At headquarters, a Retail Operation Director
- If the company is structured by country, a Country Manager
- If the company is structured by store clusters, a Cluster Manager (the cluster being a certain number of stores that are his or her responsibility)

Then, within a store, the organization will depend on the size of the store

- For a small store (less than 10 to 15 staff members) three positions are standard: Store Manager, Assistant Store Manager, Sales Expert (senior and junior may be designated).
- For a large store (30 or more employees), the Store Manager will be supported by a certain number of Assistant Store Managers aligned by function (special orders, stock, administration, service, cash desk and merchandising) or by product line (menswear/womenswear, accessories). The bigger the store and the more numerous the product lines, the more managers required.

Step 4 – The competencies

How can you identify the new luxury retail talents' aptitudes?

The aptitudes that luxury brands have come to expect from their retail teams are significantly different from what they were 15 years ago. These days they need to find talent with new competencies and aptitudes that are in-line with new challenges.

We have identified seven:

1. A high level of luxury knowledge
2. A keen sense of the art of execution (getting things done)
3. Creative and conceptual retailers: Creative and conceptual retailers are professionals who understand how to leverage brand image, customer service and quality product into a competitive advantage
4. Team builders: Retail team builders who can recruit, train, motivate and retain a productive staff
5. Sales Experts/Grands Vendeurs capable of networking with the segment of upper-echelon clientele and infiltrating the circles in which they "play and spend" all over the world
6. Hands-on executives: Hands-on store executives who can enhance revenues while controlling cost and shrinkage
7. Customer-centric thinkers: Customer-centric thinkers are able to promote crafted products, to deliver superior service and to address after-sales issues

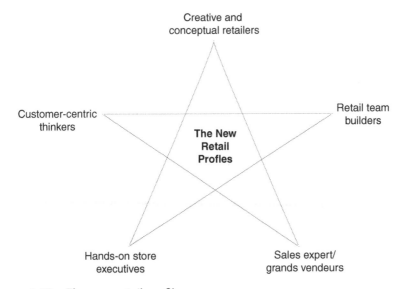

Figure 4.13 The new retail profiles

4.2.2   Managing retail recruitment

The behavioral approach

It is difficult to select and hire people who, on a daily basis, must engender a broad range of professional attitudes such as:

- Welcoming and appreciating customer needs and desires
- Explaining the craftsmanship experience to the clientele
- Dealing with client complaints and after-sales issues
- Negotiating pricing and services, when necessary

All of these attributes concern cultural background, education and personal competencies. They can be evaluated with effective interviews including a behavioral approach, which involves "behavioral" questions, such as those aimed at understanding what the candidate has done in a real situation, which may illustrate that he or she has the right competencies required for the retail job.

The behavioral approach requires significant preparation including:

- A detailed plan for each candidate meeting, specifying each competency to be investigated as well as the questions intended to measure them.
- Behavior-focused questions which should be followed up with significant probing to understand what the candidate's exact role was, and what the consequences of his or her actions were.

Examples of behavioral questions to ask

The following are key questions relevant to many retail positions, focused on behaviors, not opinions or generalities:

- Questions for evaluating **retail knowledge and experience**:
  - Describe a situation in which you invested your time to learn about a new collection/creation products. How did you proceed? What did you learn?
  - How have you maintained your knowledge of key competitors? What do you do with this information?

- Questions for evaluating **retail performance competencies**:
  - Describe the most successful commercial "deal" you negotiated. How did you achieve it?
  - When has your network of contacts really paid off for you? How did you learn from it?
  - Describe a situation in which you personally have been involved in managing a customer's complaint. What actions did you take? How did you learn from it?

- Questions for evaluating **retail personal competencies**:
  - Describe a situation in which you made an extraordinary effort to meet a deadline? What were the results?
  - How do you recharge yourself?

- Questions for evaluating **management competencies**:
  - Describe a time you led a boutique team to be more effective; what did you do?
  - How did the team and the retail organization benefit from your actions?

Case study: Recruiting a Store Director

The Brief

The company: A famous Italian fashion brand is seeking a Store Director for its strategic new flagship in Tokyo.

The mission: To successfully drive the P&L and develop the clientele with a sales and support team of about 100 people.

The expected candidate: A business manager with strong sales and public relations skills.

Status: Executive reporting to the Country Manager for Japan.

An international head hunting firm is asked to manage the search through its Tokyo office.

$\rightarrow$

The selected candidates:

- **Internal candidate:** Mitsuko W, 38 years old – dual Chinese and Japanese nationalities. She has ten years of retail experience and is considered by the brand to have "high potential" in the region. She is currently Store Director of the brand's existing boutique in Tokyo.

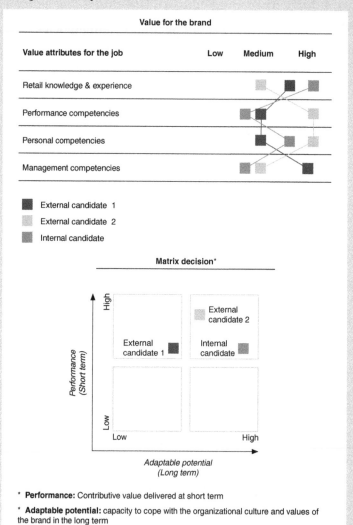

Figure 4.14   Input provided by the head hunter

→

- **External candidate 1:** Setsuko W, 45 years old – Japanese citizen 15 years of international retail management experience gained in Paris, New York and Tokyo. She currently oversees the 15 retail boutiques of an Italian leather goods company in Japan.
- **External candidate 2:** Noriko O, 42 years old – Japanese citizen. Ten years of retail experience. She has managed different boutiques in Osaka and Tokyo. For the past three years, she has managed the direct competitor's flagship.

Analysis and comments

The key point of recruiting for this position concerns behaviors that should be checked, using two major criteria

1. **Short-term candidate performance:** delivering significant added value to commercial performance, team management and daily operations.
2. **The long-term potential** of the candidate, to cope with the routine and procedures, organizational culture and the informal management systems of an Italian company.

In this case study, the material provided by the consultant lead us to the following comments:

- **Internal candidate:** Despite the fact that she has less experience, her "high potential" status within the Italian company and a positive evaluation regarding the key recruitment criteria, enable her to be a serious contender for the job.
- **External candidate 1:** Both her performance and personal competencies seem lower than those of other candidates; these factors could constitute a risk to integrating her into an Italian company.
- **External candidate 2:** Her retail operational and management experience are an asset to lead the flagship; therefore her current position at an Italian direct competitor gives her a definitive advantage.

4.2.3   Managing retail career opportunities

Developing career opportunities within the retail organization is critical for the success of store management and to minimize turnover.

Career tracks should span three organizational departments to allow sufficient flexibility: store operations, retail operations and merchandising (see Figure 4.15).

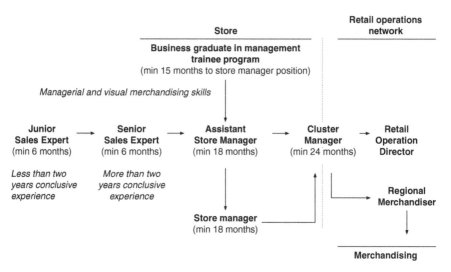

Figure 4.15   The retail career tracks

There are two levels for sales expert: junior and senior Sales Expert.

An Assistant Store Manager can be:

- Senior sales expert with extensive sales expertise as well as management and visual merchandising competencies.
- Business graduates who show good management and visual merchandising competencies and wish to make a career in retail.
- After having proven their capacity to manage a team and develop the store's performance, they will move on to Store Manager responsibilities.

Store managers will have the possibility of:

- Managing a standard store and then a flagship store
- Becoming a cluster manager after a proven track record as store manager

Clusters managers will have three possibilities:

- Retail Operations Director
- Career path into merchandising
- Career path into training

Managing a retail career

To facilitate career development, we suggest a model[6] that describes four stages in a professional's development.

This model helps HR professionals to enable development opportunities for individuals in the organization as well as identify organization-level development gaps in the talent pipeline (see Figure 4.16 for a graphic representation of these stages).

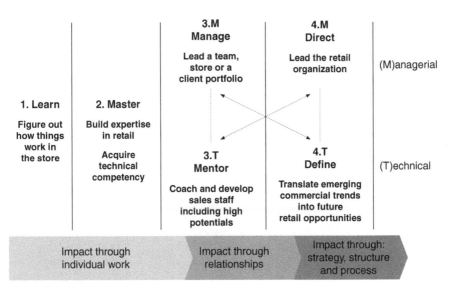

Figure 4.16   The four career development stages in retail

The career development stages help the professional define his/ her career aspirations and understand what is required for where they are now. It articulates how the stages and the track differ in the tasks that they are expected to perform, in the types of relationships they form and in the psychological adjustments they must make

- To learn, depending on others, how things work in the boutique
- To master, contributing independently, technical retail competencies
- To manage, contributing through others, a team, a store or a client portfolio
- To lead, throughout organizational leadership, the future retail developments

This career development stages model is the base for specific retail career development framework. This integrates the retail job categories that are currently available in the luxury organization and the opportunities/possible scenarios that people who want to join the retail team may have (see Figure 4.17).

In addition to these models let us look at a retail career scenario that reveals the different stages and opportunities that must be navigated in order to develop when starting as sales staff (see Figures 4.18 & 4.19).

Figure 4.17   The retail career development framework

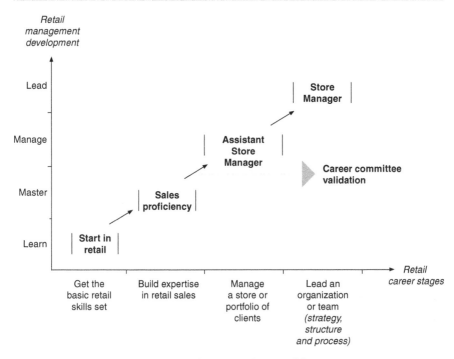

Figure 4.18 Scenario 1: start and grow in the retail function

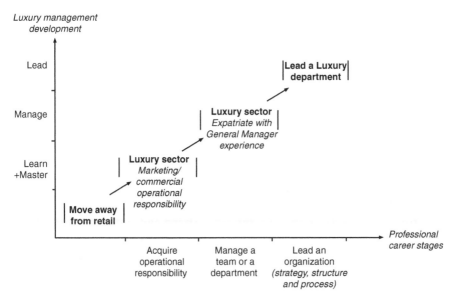

Figure 4.19 Scenario 2: moving away from the retail function

4.2.4 Designing a fair retail reward system

Three key principles must be kept in mind:

Principle 1: Redefining Rewards
The brand's retail organization must acknowledge the importance of reward programs for achieving business goals. It is a total package that includes:

- Compensation, including base pay, short-term incentives and long-term incentives
- Benefits, such as health, retirement
- Careers, including training and development, lateral moves, stretch assignments and career incentives which foster staff retention.

The total reward package is a key tool for influencing employee behaviors and attitudes, especially when a shift in business strategy requires behavioral changes.

Principle 2: Balancing Three Perspectives
Three distinct yet interrelated perspectives toned to be carefully balanced: the employer's, the employee's and the cost (see Figure 4.20).

- The Employer Perspective: our reward program engenders the knowledge, the skills and behavior necessary for business success
- The Employee Perspective: my reward is part of a compelling value proposition that understands and supports me
- The Cost Perspective: the cost of our reward scheme is affordable and sustainable and do not hinder other profitable investments.

Principle 3: Measuring return on investment
A retail organization should consider these critical questions that will help direct labor investments to maximize value:

When designing for a retail reward system, **critical Questions** (with suggested retail KPIs mentioned in italics) are to be answered.

Figure 4.20 A fair retail compensation system: balancing three perspectives

- What attributes, experience and behaviours does retail actually reward? (*Retail technical skills; "critical behaviours" for clientele; customer-data use; sales performance: high ticket sales – negotiation skills*).
- What job progressions and assignments clearly lead to successful employee performance? (*Retail stages of development; " fast tracker" career path; Apprenticeship model; etc.*).
- What are the business consequences of these employee-performance gains? (*talent-departure ratio; employee-engagement climate; employee-climate perception; customer satisfaction, etc.*).
- Which parts of the rewards package do retail employees truly value, as shown by their actions rather than their words? (*brand awareness importance; craftsmanship experience; valuable new client sales; team vs individual incentives*).
- Which retail employee segments contribute the most to business value and how? (*Store; Director; Sales Expert; other*).

When designing effective reward systems for retail, HR department and the executive committee should **focus on four key principles**:

Key Principle 1: Align each components of the compensation system with top-line organizational objectives (see Figure 4.21).

• Increase the amount of Base Pay by ending individual financial incentives (the old "eat what you kill" model) since they push sales experts to close transactions at any cost while treating team members and some customers in a destructive way (this should be adapted to acknowledge regional practices).
• Treat short-term incentives differently by relating them to the key drivers of the retail business such as employee performance, critical behaviors, customer-data collection and customer-data use.
• Promote team incentives related to the daily management of store operations and measure collective performance in order to motivate individuals to collaborate rather than to compete.
• Adjust base pay and incentives in each of the stages of retail career development.
• Provide reward and recognition solutions such as participation in a highly visible projects, participation in a mentoring program, attending a prestigious event, etc.

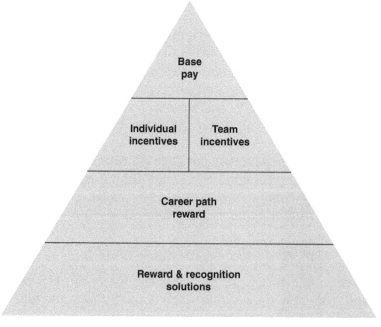

Figure 4.21 The five components of the retail compensation package

Key Principle 2: Balance the way performance is rewarded according to market and business timing (see Figure 4.22).

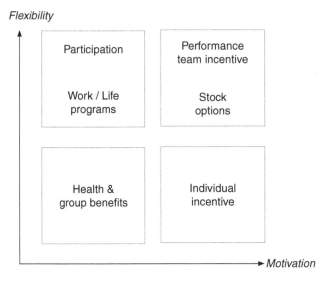

Figure 4.22 Mapping of some components Flexibility vs. Motivation

Key Principle 3: Conduct positive quarterly, mid-year and end of year reviews to keep people on the right business track. This is traditionally done in all organizations, but not necessarily for sales experts. It should be done for them too.

Key Principle 4: Benchmark your compensation system against best-in-class companies that address the same clientele (luxury competitors and Private Banking, for example).

Case study: Engineering a retail career package

This final case study illustrates how to integrate the four key principles while balancing each element when engineering a retail career package.

→

- The **risk of disagreement** between the candidate and the brand or company regarding pay and perspectives along the career path. A misunderstanding on this matter could represent a serious problem for the company and end up with a significant financial loss.
- The **main retail objectives** are those defined in the career development stages. It is important to check and to validate each job progression with the help of the career committee.
- The **career opportunities** are about job progression, specific training development and other relevant reward events that maintain employee motivation to keep them on track and help prepare the future.
- The **compensation system components** reflect career progression, balancing the importance of base pay, individual and team performances and the contribution of the management role.

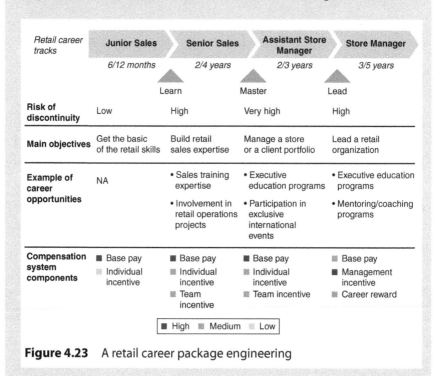

Retail career tracks	Junior Sales	Senior Sales	Assistant Store Manager	Store Manager
	6/12 months	2/4 years	2/3 years	3/5 years
		Learn	Master	Lead
Risk of discontinuity	Low	High	Very high	High
Main objectives	Get the basic of the retail skills	Build retail sales expertise	Manage a store or a client portfolio	Lead a retail organization
Example of career opportunities	NA	• Sales training expertise • Involvement in retail operations projects	• Executive education programs • Participation in exclusive international events	• Executive education programs • Mentoring/coaching programs
Compensation system components	■ Base pay ▨ Individual incentive	■ Base pay ▨ Individual incentive ▨ Team incentive	■ Base pay ▨ Individual incentive ▨ Team incentive	▨ Base pay ■ Management incentive ▨ Career reward

■ High ▨ Medium ▨ Low

Figure 4.23   A retail career package engineering

4.3 Cultivating creative/designer talent

Introduction

Luxury brands are about creation and designers. New product design is a top-down process which begins in a designer's imagination. Whatever the brand, be it with a famous Designer, a Creative Director coordinating in-house designers or a group of freelancers, designers are involved.

Because the creative element is so strong, it is often assumed that identifying, evaluating, recruiting and managing lead design is largely an intuitive and unique process, with few precedents and no guarantee of success.

However, having worked closely with creatives/designers, we have identified specific characteristics that are critical to know, providing insights for their effective recruitment and management.

4.3.1 Understanding what creatives/designers are about

The critical importance of creative teams and designers requires some non-traditional leadership and managerial skills. Leading and recruiting creative people is one of the greatest challenges facing luxury brands today. It requires huge personal sacrifice and humility on the part of leader, but it is also one of the most satisfying roles a leader can fulfill because it is ultimately about working with extremely talented individuals who are capable of incredible things.

To achieve that, it is crucial to have a clear knowledge and understanding of the specifics of their works their way of thinking, and their need to be handled with a "light" touch.

Based on experience and literature we are able to list the main characteristics of creative people; the six things a leader needs to know about creatives/designers:[7]

1. **They are paradoxical people;** they rebel against conformity and simultaneously are very attuned to whatever is happening in the environment.

2. **They are truly inquisitive, very intuitive and are acutely attuned to weak signals;** they notice things that would be unconsciously screened out by others – they can recognize patterns where others hear cacophony and because of their sensitivity they can identify stimuli around them.
3. **They are persistent and compulsive;** they have enormous amounts of energy and will power and are driven by a "magnificent obsession" toward distant goals (*their creation outcome is often a long series of advances and setbacks*).
4. **They ignore corporate hierarchy and are not afraid to take risks;** they are autonomous and independent daring to be different; they do not feel a need to "fit-in."
5. **They have a high tolerance for ambiguity (tension, suspense, unresolved questions, etc.);** conversely they are prone to anxiety (*perhaps because they are always dissatisfied with what they produce*).
6. **They won't thank you;** these creative individuals feel that they don't need to be led.

It is therefore important to understand that the Creatives/Designers who lead a brand are good at complex tasks, at being subtle interfaces between tasks and at a wide range of creative skills. In addition, they assume the particular relationships they have with the organization they work for and are not impressed by hierarchy.

Typically creative/design leaders need to work with other clever people in order to generate new products and knowledge. In many cases, they are actually motivated by working with those who may be even cleverer than they are. That's one of the reasons they need organizations. There are also pragmatic reasons. They need resources and they need organizations as a platform to achieve recognition. It's interesting to note that when looking for creative directors, LVMH looks for people who are not just creatively brilliant but who want to be famous.

4.3.2   Recruiting creatives/designers

Recruiting is a very difficult task. According to our own experience, casting (a more appropriate word in certain cases[8]) a creative/designer for a luxury brand could fail if you don't understand their distinctive attributes.

The four designer profiles

In addition the "Aristocratic Designer" and the "Street Wise Designer" and The Essence of Creation described in Part 1- section 3, one should be familiar with four distinct types of designer personality profiles that are distinguished by a specific set of characteristics: stars, creators, design marketers and young designers.

- **Stars:** these aristocratic designers bring a strong personal influence to fashion, luxury and design history by creating both their own conceptual space and their creative and aesthetic vision of the world. Thanks to their distinctive creative accomplishments they became trend setters who are highly connected to cultural and social developments all over the world.

  As previously mentioned, these artists do not necessarily draw, or possess technical competencies. They build an intellectual universe and need a close and devoted team to interpret this universe into concrete collections. They are icons; their names are equated to styles and have a place in history.

  Jean Paul Gaultier, Coco Chanel, Christian Lacroix, Karl Lagerfeld are examples among the Star designer type.

- **Creators:** artists driven by an aesthetic inspiration and/or emotional influence who have gained exceptional technical "savoir faire" and design aptitude. Very often, they will have started their creative path close to a great mentor.

  Supported by their impressive technical knowledge, their skill is to reinvent an aesthetic and dreamlike world for each collection. Starting from there, they create brands based on craftsmanship which is at the core of their brands' DNA.

  Marc Jacobs, Muccia Prada, Viktor & Rolf are part of this designer type profile.

Figure 4.24 Four designer profiles

- **Design Marketers:** designers capable of interpreting, reinterpreting or simply prolonging the codes that have been created in the past by what we have called Star or Creator designers; they have an open mindset, pick ideas and trends and have a very good understanding of a brand's DNA

   Gianfranco Ferré and Nicolas Ghesquière are Design Marketers.

- **Young Designers:** individuals who freely reinterpret fashion codes, aesthetics and style, inspired by the street, mixing ages and social and artistic heritages to create their own conceptual vision of the future.

   Business aspects, like merchandising and commercial success, are important in their creative process. They are therefore very well connected, always in touch with the luxury/fashion community and have social media skills.

   Alexander Wang, Ann Valey Hash, Damir Dorma, Alexis Mabille are some examples of this young designer type.

Case study: Recruiting a Design and Development Director

The Brief

The company: An Artistic Director, owner and CEO of a famous US fashion brand is seeking for its stylistic and design function a Design and Development Director to create and lead a strategic new men's collection.

The mission: To define the stylistic direction for the new collection while respecting the brand's aesthetic heritage and the business objectives. To monitor the development of the collections in cooperation with an in-house studio of creatives/designers (accessories, RTW, shoes).

The expected candidate: A creative, able to act as a brand-keeper, and a man or woman with strong stylistic/aesthetic codes and management focus and skills.

The status: Executive reporting to the Artistic Director, CEO of the company.

An international search agency, with offices in Milan, New York, Paris and Shanghai, has been appointed to seek the Design and Development Director.

The selected candidates:

- **Candidate 1:** Shihoro P, 28 years old – dual American and Chinese nationalities. A graduate from Central Saint Martin's School in London, where he received the Vogue and IHT Award for his men's collection in collaboration with an Asian retail fashion group.

  Currently a freelance designer working for a small number of fashion and luxury brands.

- **Candidate 2:** Alan K, 32 years old – American. Never having received a design diploma, he spent seven years as the right

→

hand of the Artistic Director of a US accessories fashion brand where he learnt the very specific procedures related to both men's and women's collections.

For the last two years he has been responsible for a men's line creative studio in Paris, New York and Tokyo.

- **Candidate 3:** Costanza A, 35 years old – Italian. A graduate from The Creative Academy in Milan with a Business Diploma from the Bocconni Young Executive Program. She has 12 years of experience in all the design jobs and activities for an Italian fashion brand.

  For the past three years she has been managing the entire design and development of both Men's and Women's collections for the Italian fashion brand.

Analysis and comments

Finding the right design and development leader is a real challenge in this case study for two particular reasons:

1. The Design and Development Director must not only embody the Men's collection in a stylistic and aesthetic sense.
2. He must however also be able to act as business partner with the CEO, who is the owner of the company; a requirement that is not obvious.

The recruitment consultant's role is critical in this particular case by providing relevant elements and accurate recommendations, tailored to the client's situation, in order to ultimately maximize the brand performance:

- Specific information about the candidates that could represent value for the fashion label include: the individuals' story, behavioral and personal competencies and his/her personal experience, style/aesthetic influences and vision for the brand.
- Additional support: detailed induction program, personal coaching during the key phases of the Men's collection agenda and suggestions for specific resources.

→

Considering the key elements above, both Candidate 1 and 3 have the cultural background and personal experience which could "fit" with the global client situation.

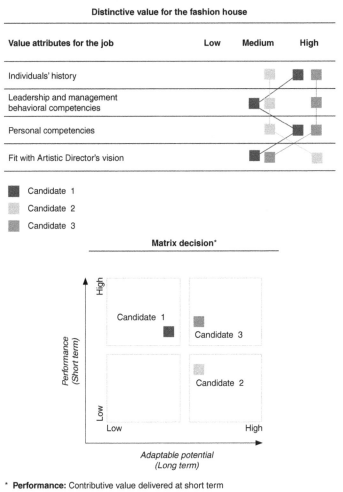

Figure 4.25 Input provided by the consultant

4.3.3 Five key principles for seeking creative/design talent

Seeking, assessing and recruiting creative/design talent remains a permanent concern for number of luxury brands. In order to address this challenge with the right approach we have designed the five following key principles:

Key Principle 1: Assess the competencies of creative/design talent comprehensively:

As with other positions in the company, the competencies of creative/design talent can be assessed along relevant parameters. The three areas to look at are:

1. **The creative/design talent's personal history.** This provides information about his/her qualifications, technical knowledge and skills, particular functional competencies and personal experience including language and cultural fluency.
2. **The creative/design talent's achievements.** Leadership and management competencies can be assessed by the way he/she effectively performs in his/her a creative role in a a current or previous organization and how he/she helps the business meet its strategic and operating objectives.
3. **The creative/design talent's personality.** This includes characteristics such as personal traits, motivation, values and personal style – all of which are significant for assessing any executive candidate but which have particular bearing on the success of individuals leading creative functions.

Key Principle 2: Scrutinize aesthetic style as a competence.

Three main things can be done to achieve this:

1. The specific blend of creative skills that a particular individual could bring to a brand must be evaluated against his/her style, culture, brand story and the objectives of the organization's ownership.
2. The evaluation of the key influencers, personal experience and educational background are critical to discovering and understanding the creative roots of an individual resulting

ability to fit with the vision of the historic founder and the characteristics of the brand's DNA.

3. Mapping the designer's profile against the four types we described earlier (see Figure 4.24) could be a determining factor.

Key Principle 3: Know the destination brand including company culture, organization and strategy development.

Finding the right creative/design profile means first knowing what the destination is all about.

As we have seen in previous sections, luxury companies must constantly maintain a dual perspective: looking backward to preserve and revitalize the essence of the brand's DNA (founding vision and heritage, craftsmanship experience and "savoir faire") while at the same time looking forward for new ideas, trends and markets.

Strategy for such companies is always a balancing act between tradition and modernity in terms of positioning, geography, markets and competition.

Thus, the creative function does not require the same skills, content, role and experience. These are just some of the challenges that must be clearly considered and articulated in developing the role and mission that the design talent is recruiting for.

Key Principle 4: Match an appropriate leadership duo.

Context is key: Is the company driven by creative vision versus a marketing/commercial focus? Who are the stakeholders?

Typically, in family-owned business, like Prada or Armani, the Artistic Director is also the owner and CEO. This exposes the company to a host of sensitive issues and potential pitfalls when the times comes to succession planning.

When the CEO and/or the Artistic Director are recruited externally the brand's future depends on the cohesiveness of this duo. A good relationship is vital for sharing a common vision which serves the same objective to maintain and develop the business and the brand. Part 3 explored this in more detail.

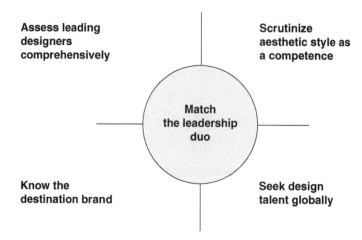

Figure 4.26   Key principles for recruiting design talent

Key Principle 5: Seek design talents globally.

Design talent is distributed across the major international fashion centers of the world: Paris, Milan, New York, London, Tokyo, Honk Kong and, these days, Shanghai. That is why many leading designers do not share the nationality or cultural background of the company they represent.

Top design schools attract students from all over the world and people who pursue design careers actively seek the experience of working and studying abroad (learning cultural and social differences along the way).

Not only is the talent pool genuinely international, but such cosmopolitanism is also a prerequisite for understanding fashion and luxury conscious consumers around the world, and drawing inspiration from many cultures.

4.3.4   Leading creatives/designers effectively

Experience has shown us that creative teams and designers are inspired by leaders they respect and admire.

Creatives /Designers expect several key and uncommon functions from the leaders they partner with: management expertise to supplement their creativity; recognition and reward delivered with a great attention; space and resources to energize their work; relevant protection against the administrative "machinery" of the organization; overall help and support when they have failed.

For this specific population three things are critical.

1. Executives should **identify mentors**, whose responsibility is to work with creatives/designers and embed their activity into a goals oriented mindset and specific budget constraints, when necessary.
2. **Foster peer network** to facilitate a sense of solidarity and a unique fertile environment in which ideas can be exchanged and hope instilled.
3. Creatives/designers should have a **specific competency – a mix of creation and commercial sense** – encapsulated in the following quote from Bernard Arnault, Chairman of LVMH: *"Designers are artists, but artists who have to make sales ..."*

As a comprehensive and practical tool for leaders of creatives/ designers, we have designed a list of "do's" and "don'ts" (see Figure 4.27 adapted from a recent book by Rob Goffee and Gareth Jones[9]).

Tell them what: Creative people don't need to be told – and generally won't be told – how to get something done. What they need is instructions on what they need to get done. It's about establishing goals and objectives rather than instructing them on how to accomplish them.

Use expertise: Creative people don't expect a leader's knowledge to match their own unique and specific know-how; they do expect that the leader is clearly and demonstrably an expert in his/her own field of expertise that supplements their own.

Give them space and resources: Creative people need workshops, equipment, libraries, specialized facilities and all the other expensive resources they crave; they perceive their own work to be so important that it must be well resourced. They are prone to obsession with perfection; it is from their obsession that brands can generate the most value and best creations.

DO	DON'T
Explain and persuade	Tell people what to do
Use expertise	Use hierarchy
Give them space and resources	Allow them to burn out
Give recognition (amplify achievements)	Give frequent feedback
Protect them from administrative rain	Expose them to politics
Create a galaxy	Recruit a star
Accept the inevitability and utility of failure	Train

Figure 4.27   Tips for managing creatives

Give recognition (amplify their achievements): What creative/ designer people do is central to their identity so recognizing their achievements is vital, but the way the recognition is delivered **from whom** and **how often** could be crucial for them.

Protect them from the rain: Very often Creative/Designer people see the administrative machinery of the organization as a distraction from their value adding activities. They therefore need to be protected from organizational "rain" and shielded from all aspects of bureaucracy.

Create a galaxy: In order to be comfortable and effective in their creative work, Creatives/Designers require a peer group of like-minded individuals; who they can team up with and be inspired by. The leadership challenge is to ensure that these Creatives/ Designers are connected to each other in ways that influence the entire organization.

Accept the inevitability and utility of failure: Creative/Designer people can be weak and vulnerable when they fail; leaders can help in this matter by providing psychological safety to maximize learning from what went wrong, recognizing the different kinds of failure and how they can be used to create mechanisms for filtering ideas and killing dead-end creative projects.

4.4 Addressing the digital age

4.4.1 The digital age: an opportunity for luxury brands

"Burberry: the best of British Digital Innovation" heralded the *Huffington Post* in November 2011. That February, Burberry Autumn/Winter 2011 women's wear show was livestreamed from Kensington Gardens onto the iconic 32m screen in Piccadilly Circus – an industry first. That livestream was viewed by over one million people online in more than 185 countries, while most fashion brands were showing to a few hundred people perched on uncomfortable bench seats in a tent.

Christopher Bailey, the Burberry chief creative officer, is just as focused on the company's digital output as he is on developing the next collection. Thanks to him the young old brand is considered as the most digitally advanced fashion brand in the world.

Bailey says: *"Burberry is now as much a media-content company as we are a design company, because it's all part of the overall experience. It's very important to consider new technologies with a light approach. Facebook, for example, is not just a mailbox. You need to keep it going, add content, create a genuine, non-deceptive relationship."*

Unlike many old-school fashion brands, notably the big Italian and French houses that have yet to fully embrace e-commerce, Burberry appreciates that we live in a digital world, and that their customers are constantly connected to the web – and each other.

"Fashion is supposed to be about making things relevant. Yes, it is luxury. Yes, it is aspiration. Yes it is supposed to be inspiring. But I think there is nothing more inspiring than talking digitally because you can get attitude, you can get music, you can get sound, you can get video and movement. You can actually articulate so much of your brand using this medium," he adds.

Likewise, as Bain & Company's 2011 luxury goods worldwide market survey, demonstrates, online luxury shopping is becoming a more relevant channel each year (see Figure 4.28)

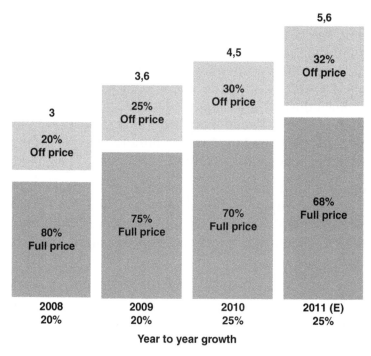

Figure 4.28 Online Luxury goods figures (in $US billions)

Bain & Company identifies four critical dimensions for the luxury goods industry:

1. Luxury shopping accounts for more than 3 percent of total online sales and could represent 5.6 percent by 2011 (estimate).

2. Increasing influence of social media and digital marketing activities improve customer experience and positively affect online sales of luxury goods.
3. Mono-brand websites and powerful multi-brand sites are enhancing customer loyalty with convenience, strong editorial content, and excellent service levels.
4. "Private sales" websites are gaining market share within the off-price[10] segment.

Although luxury brands have been investing in digital as a major communication and/or distribution channel, their attitude toward the web remains somewhat complex. Several reasons can explain this: cultural background, a new business model that focuses on customer aspirations and the generation gap.

Figure 4.29 shows the intricacies of the love/hate relationship luxury brands have with modern communications and demonstrates how luxury brands and digital environments are so different: the *virtual* issue versus *control* issue, the cultural and

Luxury brands	*Versus*	Digital world
Material products and sensory experience		Virtuality
Control and consistency are essential		Free speed and absence of control
Each brand is based on specific cultural background		No boundaries or borders; a global media
Time is an essential issue		Speed is of the essence
"Old generation"		"Young generation"

Figure 4.29   Cultural background of luxury brands and the digital world

Source: Adapted from Michel Chevalier and Michel Gutsatz (2012): *Luxury Retail Management*, Wiley & Sons.

communication philosophy, the time factor and the generation factor that pits baby boomers and generation X against generation Y.

The Net-a-porter.com case study

In 2009, the Richemont Group acquired www.net-a-porter. com, considered to be one of the most successful e-business fashion companies. Nathalie Massenet, Founder and Chairman of NET-A PORTER, pursued the company's growth strategy by seeking and launching further innovative initiatives that will continue to raise the bar in terms of online user experience.

In the 2011 Richemont Group annual report and accounts, she illustrates several key accomplishments that explain her vision and the business achievements for the brand.

Excerpts of her statement to the group shareholders:

"Since its launch in June 2000, NET-A-PORTER.COM has established itself as the world's premier online luxury fashion retailer, successfully blending content and commerce...
...With an acclaimed editorial format, leading designers, iconic packaging, unrivalled service and customer care, NET-A-PORTER enables visitors to shop over 350 designer collections 365 days a year and delivers to 170 countries with same day delivery in London and Manhattan from its own distribution centres...
...The award-winning website continuously seeks innovative ways to improve the user experience through new technology including ground-breaking interactive collaborations, shopping apps for all mobile devices, including a much-lauded weekly magazine app for the iPad that has been downloaded by over 116 000 iPad users.

$\rightarrow$

...In April 2009 the NET-A-PORTER group launched THE OUTNET, the chicest fashion outlet shopping destination. Each month, the two sites speak to more than 4 million style-conscious consumers around the world.

...February 2011 saw the launch of the first dedicated global menswear retail site: MR PORTER. The site provides a selection of the best in men's style from global designer labels to niche brands alongside editorial and style advice.

...NET-A-PORTER's technological innovations during the year have embraced new digital possibilities. The Fashion Fix provides a hub for NET-A-PORTER's social activities and is open to the public for adding comments. The mobile enabled website enables customers to browse and shop from their mobile phones.NET-A-PORTER Tv houses video content and enables customers to watch, shop, comment, embed and share. Its Google Tv extension is already available in the US for T-commerce.

...NET-A-PORTER's customer base is spread worldwide. Whilst being rooted in the UK and US, the number of customers in newer markets such as Australia, Hong Kong and France doubles each year ..."

This case study is a good example of one of the four brand web strategies, as shown in Figure 4.30. With its founding principle "to create the balance between content and commerce" Net-a-Porter has built a customer relationship based on the "conversation" adopting a "Mono-channel" strategy.

Four key lessons from NET-A- PORTER.COM

The NET-A-PORTER.COM business model is successful because it is built around four strategic advantages that ensure online user experience and satisfaction

- **Lesson 1** – Creating **exclusive collections** and one off items, created by leading designers, sold only on the Net-a-Porter web site and promoted through special and dedicated events.

$\rightarrow$

- **Lesson 2** – Giving customers **the information they want in a magazine-like format** compelling and entertaining, with permanent links to the shop and accessible through different media (web, iPad and mobile).
- **Lesson 3** – Providing **social network connections** and web communities (Facebook page, Twitter and YouTube accounts, etc.) that allow users to interact and enter dialogue with the brand.
- **Lesson 4** – Using **technology that is fully controlled in house** to ensure that end-users receive the best service, delivery and care.

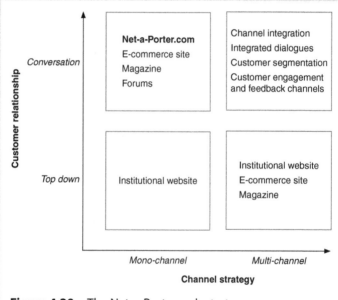

Figure 4.30   The Net-a-Porter web strategy

Source: Adapted from Michel Chevalier and Michel Gutsatz (2012): *Luxury Retail Management*, Wiley & Sons.

4.4.2   Digital Marketing structure: a framework for luxury

The organizational structure of digital operations is continuing to evolve. One of the more significant questions is the degree to which luxury brands integrate these operations into the broader corporate structure.

As we saw in previous sections, the standard organizational chart of a luxury brand splits Sales from Marketing and sometimes even from Communications, which will normally report directly to the Artistic Director. In order to address the demands of their internet savvy customers, luxury brands should rethink their business model by first identifying and segmenting its core customers and their needs, then defining the brand experience(s) to be shared with them and only then building its offering and the relevant business model. The following Marketing Digital structure framework is based upon these key critical dimensions (see Figure 4.31):

- The framework is focused on the customer experience. Placing the customer at the center of strategic and tactical decision making allows the brand to break down organizational silos and overcome persistent operational and resource issues.

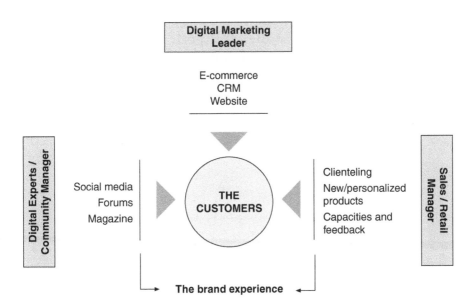

Figure 4.31 The marketing digital organization: a focus on customer experience

- Both brick-and-mortar stores and the digital world are considered simultaneously because they ensure the customer/user a complete and consistent brand experience – each locus complementing the other.
- Digital Marketing Leader, Community Manager/digital experts and Retail Managers are the key people in this digital organization.
  - Marketing is less about pushing brand messages and more about building brand intimacy through ongoing dialogue with customers and users.
  - Community managers should strive to listen and inspire and ensure that digital interactions with customers are respectful, relevant and responsive.
  - Retail managers remain focused on clienteling, presenting new/personalized products, listening to customers' experience and providing feedback to marketing.

Last but not least the digital marketing organization develops new skill-sets that bridge traditional retail with digital expertise, allowing those who did not grow up with digital to learn about the digital technologies and the opportunities they present (web communities, social media, mobile devices). We therefore suggest that the digital expert, reports to the CEO and brings his/her digital "savoir faire" to all particular projects led by Marketing, Sales/Retail, Communication and other functions (see Figure 4.32).

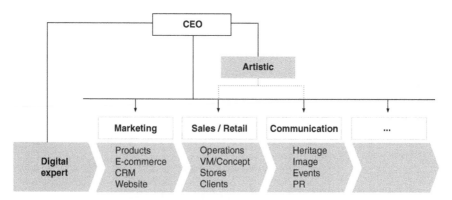

Figure 4.32 The luxury organization chart including digital expert

4.4.3 Attracting talent with skill-sets that bridge traditional and digital expertise

We believe that talent remains a significant and a particular challenge for most luxury companies that want to manage a digital strategy and/or develop new skill-sets for the digital challenges ahead.

Here are our key suggestions to consider before attracting digital talent:

1. Seek digital talent that help "migrate the digital immigrant"

On one hand you have the digital native, in his or her early 30s or younger – who grew up with digital technologies and is entirely fluent in their use; on the other hand is the "digital immigrant" who did not grow up with the Internet or mobile phones.

According to the digital media director of a well-known luxury brand, *"It's really difficult to talk to one generation in the vocabulary of another. And for digital expert to really take root, at least in the luxury industry, it's going to require existing leaders to take a leap of faith and buy into some concepts that they don't fully understand."*

In other words, the challenge is to find those who have strong abilities as an "evangelist for digital" with top level credibility – to team up with experienced senior leaders who have successfully lead the traditional luxury business models – and show them how to use these technologies and train themselves to see the commercial possibilities that arise from digital.

2. Hire those who have cultural fit for luxury

"Many digital specialists come from start-ups and have trouble adjusting to bigger organizations, normally exiting after one or

two years. Most of these mis-hires had problems moving from a free-flowing, highly intense startup culture into a corporate environment, where they had to cope with leadership challenges, hierarchies, formal processes and slower decision making," the Digital Media Director of a well-known luxury brand told one of the authors.

The culture shock can go both ways. Mis-hires at companies with advanced digital capabilities typically are those from traditional backgrounds who struggle to adjust to the intense pace and speed of decision making of an Internet business.

The challenge is assessing candidates' cultural fit with the luxury organization, which can depend on factors such as the scale and strategic importance of the digital business, how the business is organized, the level of resourcing available, how decisions are made, the pace of activity and the degree of senior-level support for digital initiatives.

At the same time, organizations should identify and check the candidate's aspiration against the peculiarities of the luxury business that we described in previous sections: the founder vision and heritage, the brand's DNA, the essence of creation, the importance of the retail function, the time factor etc.

3. The ideal is to build highly diverse teams representing digital and traditional business experience

The ideal leadership profiles are those who speak both the language of traditional retail and the language of digital, but those profiles are so rare and it is easier to compensate by building such diverse competencies within a team.

The challenge is to build a strong team with diverse experience and viewpoints who can help the organization think through the opportunities and challenges before it.

Considering the above Digital Marketing structure we believe that seeking digital creative thinkers able to team up with creative and conceptual retailers and/or train up the hands-on store executives about the digital skill-sets could be a way to successfully address the customer brand experience.

One of the art pieces commissioned by Dior from Chinese artists (in front of Plaza 66, Shanghai, 2010)

PART 5

Looking forward: luxury and China

5.1 The special characteristics of luxury in China

Greater China (Mainland China, Hong Kong & Macau) was rated in a recent Bain study (China Luxury Study 2011) as the world's no.3 market for luxury goods in the world – just behind Japan. Many observers believe that China will overtake Japan soon, if it hasn't already. Regardless of when this happens, European luxury brands should tread carefully when approaching the Chinese luxury market.

Three issues deserve careful consideration:

The real size of the Mainland China luxury market is hardly larger than the UK's: Chinese customers still largely buy their luxury goods outside Mainland China – either in Hong Kong/Macau or when traveling to Europe. In 2012 Bain reports that Chinese luxury customers spent 28 percent of their luxury budget overseas, 34 percent in Hong Kong/Macau and only 38 percent in Mainland China (down from 43.5 percent in 2009). This means that although the Chinese are luxury's no. 2 customers in the world, Mainland China isn't. This is linked to the significant price differences that exist between Mainland China and the rest of the world[1]:

- The University of International Business and Economics in China reported that the price of luxury watches sold in China were 161 percent higher than those sold abroad.

- A survey conducted by the Ministry of Commerce (MOFCOM) revealed that the prices of 20 luxury brands over five categories, namely watches, leather goods, apparel, liquor and electronic products, were approximately 45 percent, 51 percent and 72 percent higher than those sold in Hong Kong, the United States and France, respectively.

It is assumed that current import taxes on luxury goods will be lowered in the coming year. However, luxury brands are known to keep prices high in some overseas market – a policy that has been successful in Japan for years. There is therefore no reason to think that the most important brands will lower their prices in Mainland China if taxes are reduced.

Some luxury brands may be overstretching themselves in China: Boss has 139 stores, Armani 119, Dunhill 107, Montblanc 101. A recent paper in WWD (Dunhill's China Challenge, March 20, 2012) states that 40 percent of Dunhill's customers are now Chinese but that the brand is losing its identity and its sense of direction. "I recall seeing Dunhill points of sale in smaller, mid-end department stores, selling polo shirts, belts and other accessories that did not really seem to be in line with the brand image they want to convey," said a person interviewed. "They are going downhill," said an executive of one of China's leading high-end department store chains. "They are either going to have to close some stores and become top tier or just have a lot of stores and go for sales. We consider them a second-tier brand. They are everywhere, they have lost their exclusivity." Figures are the best way to understand the danger that awaits these luxury brands : Dunhill has 13 stores in Beijing , 5 in Chengdu and 3 in Kunming. Brands like Aquascutum, Armani, Cerrutti 1881 (now owned by Li & Fung), Zegna, Gieves & Hawkes have gone the same way. What about the major luxury brands? Louis Vuitton only has 42 stores; Cartier, 37; Hermès, 20; and Chanel, 8. Contrary to these famous brands, the brands we are mentioning here (Dunhill, Aquascutum, etc.) can soon be viewed more as middle-tier fashion brands than brands that are meant to be the embodiment of European luxury.

There is a huge talent shortage in China when it comes to salespeople: With luxury brands opening stores at the rate of more than 150 per year (meaning 6 to 20 salespersons per additional store, which equates to around 2000 to 3000 new salespersons per year) and a new focus on second and third tier cities, the talent pool is shrinking rapidly. Meanwhile, Chinese customers are amongst the most demanding in the world when it comes to service. Luxury brands are therefore faced with multiple challenges including people that do not show up for interviews (up to 30 percent!), poor motivation, poor service skills, rising demand for better pay – without necessarily aiming long-term career goals. All of this is well documented and some luxury brands are trying to meet this challenge: the Richemont Group recently opened a Retail Academy in Shanghai and Starwood is creating a mentoring program for its Chinese workers. All luxury brands will need to maintain consistent service levels throughout China if they wish to keep their upscale luxury image and satisfy the demands of their Chinese customers – who may decide to go overseas to get the level of service they seek.

5.2 The key brand competencies the Chinese need to acquire

5.2.1 Chinese companies purchase European premium & luxury brands – but do they have the brand management skills to develop them?

In 2011 and 2012, three successive acquisitions occurred of European luxury brands by Fung Brands Limited – an investment fund (attached to Fung Capital Europe) owned by Victor and William Fung:

- The acquisition of 80 percent of Sonia Rykiel, the famous French fashion brand (with annual sales of 90 million Euros in 2010). The brand has 365 employees and manages 65 stores and is sold mostly through wholesale.

- The acquisition of an 80 percent share in Delvaux, the Belgian leather goods manufacturer, through DLX Holdings, an ad-hoc subsidiary of Fung Brands Ltd. Founded in 1829 in Brussels, since 1883 Delvaux has been an appointed supplier to the Court of Belgium. The brand has three production facilities in Brussels, in Bourg-Argental (France) and Ho Chi Minh City (Vietnam). The company operates 10 stores of its own, and has 220 employees with an annual sales turnover of 17 million Euros.
- The acquisition of 90 percent of Robert Clergerie through a subsidiary, RC Holdings of Fung Brands Ltd. The brand has around 200 employees, independently manages a network of 20 stores all over the world and has a manufacturing workshop and a development center in Romans (its original birthplace, near Grenoble). Its annual turnover represents over 20 million Euros.

Chinese companies are purchasing European brands, a phenomenon that started about five years ago.

- Examples abound in the automotive industry: In 2005 Nanjing Auto bought MG, and SAIC (Shanghai Automotive Industry Corporation) acquired the rights of several Rover models. These were redeveloped and marketed under the name Roewe, with great success. Since SAIC's subsequent acquisition of Nanjing Auto, the new group re-launched the MG in Britain in 2009/2010, with models that were well received by critics. The group's portfolio also comprises the rights to Austin Healy, purchased in 2007. In 2010, Geely bought Volvo from Ford.
- In 2008, Weichai Group, the first Chinese manufacturer of boat engines, trucks and construction equipment, bought Moteurs Baudoin – recognized experts in marine engines. In 2012 they finalized the acquisition of Ferretti – the world's largest manufacturer of luxury yachts, with brands like Riva and Ferretti to their credit.
- A similar phenomenon is appearing in fashion. In 2008, the Hembly International group bought Sergio Tacchini. In 2009, Zhongfu bought the rights to Pierre Cardin in China. In 2010 Shandong Ruyi (the world leader in spinning and weaving, one of the Hugo Boss sub-contractors) acquired 41 percent of the

Japanese fashion company, Renown, and, the Italian clothing company, Tombolini.

So far, Chinese companies have been building on the low-cost business model: Low prices made the difference, and some even resorted to dumping to get rid of competitors in the market. They have now clearly understood that owning a brand generates higher margins than being a manufacturer for the brand's owner. This explains why over 20 percent of company heads surveyed in a recent study by The Economist[2] say they are in search of brands.

This movement is part of the major overseas direct investments made by (mostly private) Chinese companies since 2004, which is, according to the only study available on the topic, "dominantly motivated by seeking technology and other strategic assets – mainly brand names."[3]

However, Chinese companies are faced with significant managerial shortcomings, especially where integration of foreign teams and marketing are concerned. The Economist's survey shows that Chinese companies acquired 298 foreign companies in 2009 (including 13 percent in Europe and 13 percent in the U.S.), but only 39 percent of top managers surveyed believe they have the skills to integrate these acquisitions. The challenges ahead are therefore significant.

"Chinese multinational companies rarely have firm-specific ownership advantages—notably, core technology, organisational and management skills, and brand names."[4] This lack of management skills is nowhere more evident than in the development of global brands. Brand management competencies and skills are not part of the Chinese business culture. As Y.C. Yeh, founder of Tai Ping carpets said *"The Chinese are very good at manufacturing, but the culture forbids marketing."*[5] Many important dimensions of brand management have yet to be mastered, including building brand consistency, respecting intellectual property rights, pricing, quality control, applying a contract-based culture, managing creators and designers and building affluent customer relationship.

These competencies can be learned through partnerships with European brands and experts. There are three main methods to achieve this:

1. **Buy European luxury brands and create mixed teams with a European CEO** (Fung Capital went this route – appointing Jean-Marc Loubier, former marketing Director of Louis Vuitton and former CEO of Escada, as the CEO of their new acquisitions);
2. **Adopt the Artistic Director/CEO or COO model** of mixing cultures in which a duo manages the brand – one being Chinese, the other being European, for example, Guillaume Brochard, French, Founder/CEO and Dennis Chan, Chinese, Founder/ Artistic Director, the duo behind Qeelin[6]). Another example is the development of Sheji/Sorgere – a men's luxury brand set up by China Garments with products designed by Francesco Fiordelli (Fashion Director) and manufactured by Caruso, an Italian company.
3. **Work with European branding experts** on (re)developing existing Chinese brands (an approach adopted by Herborist, a beauty brand from the Shanghai Jahwa Group).

These brand management competencies and skills are critical and will be even more so because China is in a transitional phase – moving from 'made in China' to 'designed in China' (as stated in the twelfth five-year plan adopted early 2012). Regarding textiles, the plan calls for the establishment of between five and ten internationally recognized Chinese brands and at least 100 nationally recognized brands by 2015. It also states that more brand management and brand building education should be instigated in order to bolster China's fashion industry. As Lin Yun Feng, VP Chinese Chamber of Commerce of Textile Industry said in a recent interview (January 2012): *"Chinese competitive companies will go the quality-way. They will work with European designers. I cannot exclude that those that fail to evolve in this manner will go bankrupt."*

Our advice to Chinese firms who want to create world class premium and luxury brands is simply three words: Buy / Hire / Learn.

1. Buy expensive brand management expertise and/or buy brands (and respect their business culture).
2. Hire international talent in all dimensions of brand management.
3. Learn from competitors with the help of international business schools.

5.2.2 Major luxury brand management competencies and how they are not (yet) mastered by Chinese brands

Based on our experience of working with Chinese companies, the following four real examples illustrate the gap between European and Chinese brands.

Case 1: Building brand consistency

The European luxury brand approach:

- Buy expert and creative skills for all communication objects (Leaflets, Website, advertising, etc.).
- Manage numerous egos – the Creative Director, the Photographer, the creator of the perfume bottle, the Face, etc.
- Have a dedicated internal team with required talent.

Chinese luxury brand case study 1
The Brand buys ONE brand communication object from an external creative expert. It then uses internal/local designers to create all the others.

Consequence: absence of consistency and poor quality

Chinese luxury brand case study 2
Despite having a Creative Director and an international architect for its store concept, the Brand decides to work with a local web agency to build its website.

Consequence: no core creative skills applied to the web and poor execution.

Case 2: Setting price levels

The European luxury brand approach:

- Benchmark the competition;
- Set prices based on the brand positioning and *not* on the cost structure;
- Set different prices on different markets;
- Have a dedicated internal team with required pricing talent.

Chinese luxury brand case study:
It adopts a pricing based on cost structure – with different multipliers for different products in similar lines.

It changes prices erratically – some go up, some go down, without real justification.

It prices similar objects differently, with no justification in the eye of the customer.

It has no dedicated team with required talent: the pricing is done by the CEO and the COO.

Consequence: price inconsistency and customers are lost.

Case 3: A shared international business culture

The European luxury brand approach:

- A contract-based culture: in all cases contracts are drawn (licensing contract, distribution contract, supplier contract, etc.).
- State-of-the-art compliance regulations are required.

- Dedicated internal teams with required talents (legal, marketing, etc.) exist.

Case study: the co-branding project

An international luxury brand and a Chinese luxury brand decide to produce a collection of objects, manufactured by the Chinese brand and sold in the international brand's stores but presented as a co-branding enterprise...

International luxury brand

Could you please sign our compliance regulations (code of conduct, etc.) that all our suppliers are supposed to sign?

Chinese luxury brand

We are not a supplier but a co-brander – we will not sign these papers.

International luxury brand

Please try to understand, we are buying a product from you – it is a supply chain process – our code of conduct is a document that all companies that we do business with must adhere to.

Chinese luxury brand

We have agreed that this is a co-branding project in which both brands should be in an equal position. It is unfair for you to consider us as your supplier.

You took the initiative for this project. If you really intend to keep this collaboration, you should respect our business mode. It's a handshake business – mutual trust is its basis.

International luxury brand

This transaction is not about trust – what we have to do has to be compliant to the rules and regulations as set forth by our parent company.

Chinese luxury brand

We understand that you have your rules and regulations. We have our own manners too. You should have stated that clearly when you first came to us for this collaboration: we would not have wasted our time.

International luxury brand
Please understand that the marketing team has agreed on the co-branding and still wants it. This is an issue with the legal department.

Consequence: the project is abandoned

Case 4: Managing scarcity

The European luxury brand approach:
- It manufactures products in a given country of origin.
- It benefits from the positive image of this country of origin.
- It accepts not to satisfy customer demand: it adapts the product offer to the manufacturing volume.

Chinese luxury brand case study
The brand imports very high-priced European products into China.

Facing a demand that exceeds the offer, it decides to have additional products manufactured in China and to sell them as European products.

Consequence: In its grab for short-term profits, the brand now faces customer dissatisfaction and legal complications for having broken the law.

The Tai Ping case

Tai Ping was created in 1956 – under the name Hong Kong Carpets International Limited – by Michael Kadoorie (and seven other shareholders) as a philanthropic organization, both to give work to refugees from mainland China and to safeguard China's carpet-making skills. This artisan workshop produced carpets for the Peninsula Hotel, one of the major assets of the Kadoorie family. The management was handed over to Anthony Yeh – one

$\rightarrow$

of the shareholders and a graduate in mechanical engineering from Syracuse University (USA) who developed a new technical process: the mechanization of the knotting system or "tufting" technique. Tai Ping (which went public in 1973) thereby became a manufacturing-oriented company, with factories in mainland China (Nanhai) and Thailand, targeting the hospitality market, offices, convention centers, golf and country clubs, casinos, and restaurants in Hong Kong and South East Asia. In 1989 Anthony Yeh was succeeded by his son Kent Yeh –a graduate of Berkeley (Industrial Engineering) and Wharton (MBA). Following the opening-up of China's economy, the new Managing Director decided to invest in new ventures like cosmetics, cement and bottled water, as well as a furniture rental business in Hong Kong. Tai Ping lost $HK200m divesting itself of these loss-making mainland investments from 1996 to 1998.[7] The first reorganization led the company to concentrate on its core competency: carpet making. Sales turnover for 2000 was US$56.4m (HK$439.6m). Tai Ping also started to explore the B2C market (the residential market) and was selected as a subcontractor for major designers and luxury brands wishing to develop carpet lines within their offering. In the early 2000s, for example, Tai Ping manufactured the Kenzo Maison carpets.

Nevertheless the Tai Ping's overall concentration on B2B markets (cited as "floor coverings" in their 2002 results document) led them to face a difficult situation: under the pressure of a market that was increasingly oriented towards lower-priced products, their gross margin declined steadily. Some factories in mainland China – a joint venture established in 1993 with a privatized carpet manufacturer which sold products under the Shanhua brand – proved to be operating exclusively in the more price sensitive hospitality sector.[8]

In 2003 after having brought in an external firm of management consultants, the board decided on a major strategy shift, not to mention a new Managing Director. As J. S. Dickson Leach, the Chairman wrote: "After careful consideration the Directors and I have decided that in order to grow and create shareholder value

$\rightarrow$

and long term prospects for all its stakeholders the Company must move from its previous factory oriented direction and become a customer driven business. To achieve this, it is necessary to make some fundamental changes to the way we do our business. In the second half of this year agreement was reached with the previous Managing Director for him to step down from his executive role, but for him to remain a non-executive member of the board. A search is underway for an international CEO with strong branding and sales experience. The management structure is also being changed."[9] James Kaplan, former SVP Sales and Marketing Director of Knoll International, was hired as CEO that same year.

James Kaplan's three-prong strategy to turn the company around was to invest more in its luxury products; sell off non-core assets (the furniture business in 2006 and, in 2012, the 49 percent stake in the factory in mainland China) and diversify further into the residential carpet market as a launch pad out of Asia. The firm's specialist residential carpet trade had nearly suffocated under the weight of the commercial machine-made division which had swollen over the years before Kaplan entered the frame.[10] In 2003, 90 percent of Tai Ping's sales had come from corporate clients but in 2011, thanks to a network of showrooms (the United States being the brand's primary target), residential carpet sales had climbed from 10 percent to almost 40 percent.

This was made possible by management team's internationalization and a strictly controlled branding strategy. This included the creation of a new logo and branded communication; a reorganization of the brand architecture (a new brand, "1956 by Tai Ping" was created in 2011 for the hospitality industry with a new visual identity to distinguish commercial products from residential[11] and two further brands were acquired: Edward Fields in the United States in 2005 and the Manufacture de Cogolin in France, in 2011); the opening of a US flagship in 2005; a new distribution strategy; a new pricing strategy. Today Tai Ping considers itself to be a luxury carpet company that only sells 100 percent custom-made products. This has led the company (and all its

→

brands) to distribute only through B2B channels, and never to go the BtoC way.

As James Kaplan says himself: "I've stepped back and realized that where we manufacture our product is second to how we develop the brand globally. There is often the question of, 'will a Chinese luxury brand work in Europe and the US?' I think the answer is yes as long as you maintain the standards of quality and design and customer service that people expect from a luxury brand." Sales more than doubled, going from 563 million HK$ in 2004 to 1.221 billion HK$ in 2010. Anthony Yeh and Kent Yeh resigned from the board in 2005.

This fascinating story is a perfect example of the hurdles traditional Chinese family companies face when going international. We can identify 4 major hurdles:

Hurdle 1: The manufacturing bias

Chinese companies have built their development mostly on manufacturing. When it comes to building an international presence, they remain fueled by a manufacturing mindset. They will invest in manufacturing facilities, in processes, and will stay volume and product-driven. Their instinct is to try to lower prices to gain market share.

Note 1: The Western education of its managers (even at the MBA level) does not help change this perspective. It may even lead to hazardous investments, by adding a financial bias to the manufacturing bias.

Hurdle 2: The lack of brand management competencies

Building a brand (as we have seen in this book) needs very specific competencies in image building, design management, production control, distribution control, pricing and storytelling that most Chinese companies do not have. The role played by a

$\rightarrow$

management consulting firm and the hiring of a new CEO with the appropriate experience has radically changed this at Tai Ping and allowed it to build a real luxury brand.

When James Kaplan took over he found different logos, different websites, different so-called 'brands' used in different countries. Simone Rothman, who he brought in as Chief Marketing Officer, decided to unify all this and to build a single branding strategy (with a logo, a visual vocabulary, etc.) with the help of European branding experts. Her background in design and architecture was an asset here.

Building a brand includes deciding on how to manage the brand portfolio. The decision to develop Tai Ping, Edward Field and Manufacture de Cogolin as three separate brands and not bring all products under the sole Tai Ping brand was a critical decision. It proves that each brand's heritage and characteristics are respected and that their positioning is clearly defined.

Hurdle 3: The propensity to "short cut"

Simone Rothman is adamant: "luxury is a business where no short cuts are possible."[12] She describes herself as a "control freak" which is in-line with numerous examples we discussed earlier in this book. Building a luxury brand takes time and every step must be controlled: Tai Ping's management had to enforce this when they decided to rebuild their headquarters in Hong Kong, making sure that their Chinese team consented to having all relevant details monitored by American designers and the New York team.

This leads to a fundamental contradiction to the tendency Chinese managers and executives have of looking for short-term benefits, of accepting second best, working in haste and having little respect for intellectual property. Such opportunistic behaviors conflict with the requirements of building a luxury brand.[13]

→

Hurdle 4: The Chinese family business

Business literature is replete with analyses of the cultural impact of traditional Chinese family businesses. Most of these papers underscore the importance of cultural traits that impact the way Chinese managers develop their business. Some of the major conclusions are consistent with the Tai Ping situation:

- The **importance of trust** – given mostly only to close family members and to classmates. This leads to a lack of trust in outsiders (and in professional managers).[14]
- **"Familism"**: i.e., the overriding respect for family authority and hierarchy, loyalty, commitment and contribution to the family[15]
- **Confucian dynamism**, a traditional Chinese trait, has a direct negative influence on international entry mode decisions.[16] In fact managers with strong Confucian values will adopt very conservative attitudes when faced with risk or uncertainty. Moreover they are more cautious when it comes to the costs incurred by competition when entering international markets. Decision-making is another domain where the Confucian values have a great impact : information analysis and interpretation is mainly done through relatives or potential business partners and the decision-maker's own subjective evaluations. Finally these executives will insist on their own ideas to enhance their authoritative position – although they may at some point show respect to other's suggestions to maintain a harmonious relationship. This has serious consequences : Chinese leaders with strong Confucian values may have great difficulties accepting to work with Western experts.
- **The role of the CEO:** "A CEO in the western world is normally looked upon as a consensus builder or as an individual who debates and discusses strategies with their employees and then executes the strategy, whereas in China the leader is looked upon as the sole decider and executor of strategies."[17] This once again shows the limits of possible collaborations between Chinese and Western executives when their cultural values are too far apart.

5.3   Why hiring Asian executives is essential?

The lack of Asian nationals in senior executive positions across the Asia Pacific region is a global issue for the industry. As a key player and by far the most important growth market in the region, China has become the top priority for luxury brands but the talent there is scarce. Brands will not be able to rely on luxury's most traditional recruitment technique, i.e., poaching from the competitor.

In the coming battle for talent and experience across Asia, most luxury brands will have to come up with new approaches to satisfy their requirements, something that India – the next growth market – will soon need to consider too.

The challenge in China is threefold:

• Identify local potential entrepreneurs capable of building solid and profitable distribution businesses (retail and/or wholesale) while developing the brand's notoriety and implementing the strategy and procedures of the luxury company they work for.[18]
• Train and develop a new generation of local talent at middle and junior level on the characteristics of luxury: its unique business model, the competencies and behaviors expected, the challenges of retail and merchandising, etc.
• Acquire a deep understanding of Chinese consumers and of local cultural trends in order to build specific customer relationship and customer loyalty programs.

To attract high quality executives, visible partnerships must be developed: with Universities and Business Schools, political institutions, administrations and Consulting and Communication agencies.

Likewise, in order to enable local people to remain loyal to the organization and prepare the leaders of the future, luxury brands need to provide win-win career deals including visible career paths and reward systems that encourage collaboration.

Finally, luxury brands should try to build "leadership duos," associating an Asian executive with a European/American executive. Such a leadership duo could, for instance, bring an executive talent from HQ together with a local high potential talent at middle level, with a view to having the duo learn from each other in order to succeed together in their common mission. This innovative way of cooperation requires a strong end-to-end process that identifies the right talent, selects the relevant project and audits and reviews the duo.

The following section will develop these points further, illustrated by some real examples and case studies and key recommendations on how luxury brands should tackle these challenges.

5.3.1   The talent market in China

"As China's economy continues to grow at a breakneck pace, thousands of new businesses are starting up, discretionary income is growing rapidly with the emergence of a new middle class, and wealth is being created as never before."[19] Trying to recruit and retain high-caliber talent in the luxury industry can be daunting.

What motivates a Chinese engineer (or graduate with a MBA) to work for an Italian fashion company in Shanghai? If you don't know, you risk falling behind in the race for talent in this emerging market.

Let's start with the big picture. This new market is growing so fast, even established global players aren't recruiting and retaining enough employees. For the China market two important factors are important:

1. The Cultural Revolution created a "missing generation" of those aged 45 to 55. Expatriates therefore fill the most jobs at the top.
2. Young workers are flooding the marketplace but because education quality varies greatly among schools, many of them are grossly unprepared.

The figure below, adapted from Egon Zehnder,[20] shows where deficit and surplus exist in China at four levels: entry, middle management, country leadership and regional leadership. The cross-hatched area represents the talent pool; the white area show deficit or surplus of talent.

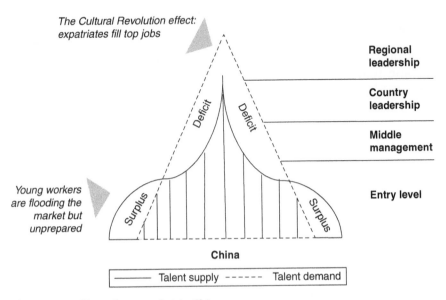

Figure 5.1   The talent market in China

The gap between employee supply and demand is especially wide when it comes to candidates capable of moving into senior leadership roles. As a result, as mentioned earlier, a great number of expatriates fill the most critical top jobs.

Likewise, many recruits fresh out of universities lack the language and other skills to take on even entry-level positions in global companies.

Furthermore, salaries in China have risen out of proportion to the expertise of the talent pool, creating unrealistic expectations among potential employees. Finally, China's one-child policy has created a unique problem. As one manager, working as Director for the Asian market for a French jeweler, told to us:

> *"Consider that millions of young Chinese have no siblings and no cousins. It's not too difficult to see how the child can become the center of attention for the entire family. It's not easy giving critical feedback to someone who is not used to it and who has lots of employment options elsewhere."*

In this context, while luxury has become a ubiquitous and massive industry in China with annual growth exceeding 50 percent for many brands, luxury talent is increasingly scarce. The luxury industry is faced with a talent bottleneck, where the talent pipeline has not kept up with growth. The context has radically changed:

- Ten years ago Cartier, Chanel, Hermès and Louis Vuitton had just a few boutiques each in China (one to five). They were often small shops inside hotels and stores owned by exclusive agents/ distributors.
- After decades of central planning, which eliminated any sign of luxury as well as the overall concept of it, China has had no luxury base of its own,

This meant that luxury brands had to bring in their own managers from overseas while they were in the startup phase. In the 90s, top management came from the brand's home country – Europe and the US – and middle management tended to be drawn from Hong Kong, Taiwan and Singapore to meet the demand for the degree of sophistication that was lacking locally. This importing of talent also limited development opportunities for local staff seeking a career path in the luxury business.

Last but not least, another factor limiting the growth of the Senior Executive pipeline has been the operational nature of the business, where strategies were decided and designed at head office and simply executed locally. That is why until recently, the demand for talent focused on execution skills rather than leadership skills.

5.3.2　Testimonials about China's talent challenges[21]

Testimonial 1 – The sector expertise

James Zhang, the President of LVMH China says "Indeed, the talent pool in China is still being developed, since the history of the luxury business sector goes back less than ten years, which is rather short. To get the right candidates, who have a strong sense of luxury and customer focus with great potential to be developed further, is far more important than to get the candidate with only a short period of luxury working experience and unproven credibility and capability in the market."

To find such skills, luxury houses need to search in sectors that teach high–quality customer service, attention to detail and the one-on-one human touch, as well as aesthetics and beauty; sectors such as high-end hospitality and cosmetics are worth considering.

Luxury brands should also look at general retail – specialty or mass retail – since these sectors have already attracted and developed a large number of brilliant mainland Chinese talent.

"In China one needs to think out of the box, take risks and come up with quick and creative solutions," says the head of a Swiss watchmaking brand who has spent the past 15 years in Hong Kong and Shanghai. So, hiring from external talent pools is a plus not a minus and it is especially true for the luxury market.

Testimonial 2 – Promote Chinese managers

According to the previous head of Richemont Group in China. "One of the key success factors for Cartier in China has been that our market-oriented functions such as sales, marketing and PR are all headed by mainland Chinese, who know and understand the fast changing needs of our Chinese customers. Ideally you can mix the local talent with westerners who have experience in Asia, deep brand knowledge and a strong entrepreneurial spirit. In general you need leaders in China who will be responsible for people and for decision making and who are ambitious about shaping the future of the brand."

Testimonial 3 – Invest on talent grooming

"Given the large number of boutiques open and opening in China in the next five years, we are facing a serious challenge to find both junior staff and senior executives. So we focus very much on training in order to cope with our expansion" notes the EVP Human Resources of Chanel.

Building the necessary mid-to-long term talent pipeline is vital. This includes training, coaching and succession planning. There needs to be a combined approach that blends knowledge and appreciation of luxury's unique culture with practical experience in a flagship or operational department in order to engrain sales, and management behaviors.

For this reason luxury brands such as Shangri La, Hermès and Richemont group launched their own training/sales academies (see the Richemont Retail Academy case study, below).

5.3.3 How can luxury brands win this Chinese talent contest?

In their HBR article Ready, Hill, and Conger[22] suggest two strategies which we have adapted to the idiosyncracies of the luxury industry described earlier in this book. These strategies are illustrated in Figure 5.2.

First strategy – Attract talent by making compelling promises

Center these promises on the **company's brand**:

- Does the luxury brand have a reputation for excellence that may lead to personal advancement?
- Does the luxury brand have a unique business model that is based on creation and craftsmanship?

Figure 5.2   Attracting and retaining Chinese talent in luxury: a framework

- Does the luxury brand have leaders that can inspire passion and trust for people?

Then focus on **the company's opportunity**:

- Will the luxury brand provide a visible career path?
- Will the luxury brand offer a continual training program?
- Will the luxury brand ensure competitive pay?

Finally explain the characteristics of the company's purpose:

- Does the luxury brand have a mission and values that are meaningful to potential new hires?
- Does the luxury brand provide its people with the right to act as global ambassadors to promote brand recognition among Chinese people?
- Does the luxury brand offer diverse projects that enable its people to grow within Asia?

Second strategy – Retain talent by keeping your promises

Craft a culture characterized by three critical things:

- A good command of English and French and/or Italian languages and knowledge of their cultures.

- Strong communication about the essence of brands, their cultural roots and craftsmanship experience, the historic collections, etc.
- Education about how to behave with luxury customers: the art of execution, the provision of superior service, the attention to detail and the human touch.

Insight – The Retail Academy of Richemont Group

In April 2012, The Richemont Group opened a Retail Academy in Shanghai with the objective of training Chinese students as luxury retail assistants for its stores across China and to wherever Chinese people travel. The Cartier, Chloé and Net-a-Porter owner will soon begin to train students in a number of professional skills and sales techniques taught by luxury industry experts and guest lecturers.

The nine week training course will involve students in market research and online activities, as well as practical assessments to gauge sales and management abilities. Nestled between high-end boutiques and flagships on Shanghai's Huahai Zhong Road, the exclusive academy will run five courses each year, with just 50 students in each class.

"The retail academy will be a long term and consistent talent development model for us. Once proven in China, more countries and cities will participate in the model. Richemont has another advantage: our worldwide networks of boutiques need Mandarin speaking sales associates. So there are opportunities for our trainees in China to learn and live their potential in overseas postings." notes Mr. Alain Li, Regional CEO at Richemont for Asia Pacific region.

5.3.4 Conclusion

In China people are trained to do well in exams and learn by rote. As the result, local employees often are considered by expatriates to lack creativity and proactivity. In contrast, citizens in western societies are trained to learn key concepts and apply those in different contexts. Western leadership, therefore, focuses more on creating a vision and empowering employees to achieve this through their own decisions and actions.

Cultural differences between the two lead to differing expectations about conduct in leadership roles. From a western viewpoint one may perceive Chinese leaders to be lacking autonomy, creativity and independent thought and to be "rule driven."

"They need to acquire leadership capabilities in order to interact with the business world: reporting added value for the HQ, communicating key messages to local business analysts and building strong relationship with shareholders" says Charles de Brabant, CEO and Founding Partner of an executive search boutique located in Shanghai. In a similar way, from a Chinese viewpoint one may find it difficult to understand what the expectations and roles of western leaders are and may perceive them to be lacking the rigor and depth needed for strong decision making and performance delivery.

That is why we need to balance different expectations in China and the West as to how leaders should behave.

When it comes to executive talent luxury brands want to attract, develop and retain what has to be done?

They should first realize that although their brands are attractive to the increasingly affluent Chinese customers they are remarkably less attractive to Chinese talent. As disclosed in interviews with local recruiters, luxury companies are seldom an employer of choice.

In a white paper[23] Philipp Haermmerle – recruitment expert at Heidrick & Struggles for the luxury and retail sectors in China –

points out the qualities that most talented Chinese executives value over "brand":

- Freedom to innovate
- Autonomy to make decisions
- Visible career development
- High level of responsibility and broad job scope
- Suitable organization (performance driven yet family-like in culture, with minimal politics)
- Bosses who motivate and coach
- Team spirit
- A track record of success

"These factors rank ahead of the brand in the majority of cases. Western brands tend to overestimate their power of attraction, which has dropped in recent years. In the meanwhile Chinese companies have become a magnet competing for the best mainland Chinese executive talent" he says.

Thus, luxury brands should attract mainland executive talent with a new perspective. Some key ideas to keep in mind are:

1. Simplify reporting structures and provide to the very entrepreneurial Chinese candidates more space and resources.
2. Demonstrate that luxury is "art of execution" throughout creative/designer and sales experts testimonials, and with the experience of craftsmanship (the luxury business is often perceived as too "executional" by Chinese executives).
3. Educate, educate and educate the wider market about the essence and the uniqueness of luxury brands.
4. Coach Chinese executives to engage the brand in corporate social responsibility and arts events.

Winning the talent war for luxury brands in China requires a great deal of effort and patience to reach an understanding of different expectations for leadership, as well as alignment on what success should look like. Innovation and participation of everyone should be critical – and a strong Chief Human Resources Officer a definitive advantage to lead this particular change.

Listening to a successful duo: The Shang Xia case[24]

What responsibilities does each of you have? In what way do you think they are complementary?

Jiang Qiong Er (CEO & Creative Director)

My background is creative, artistic. I started six years ago. I think it is very important to have real talent to specialize in management and business development. Even if I have a leaning for management I lack the techniques and experience. While it develops, I shall have to stick to my priority, which is creativity and the vision of Shang Xia, the future – what will we be doing in one year, three years, five years? In the course of time, while Shang Xia develops, the boutiques open, when the range expands, there will be more and more effort on management, as compared to today, or six years ago.

I think we need partners. I, personally, do not believe in hiring. Philippe, for me, it's not recruitment, it's a happy encounter because in this kind of story, if one wishes to remain together for a long time, it is not recruitment that is needed, but a fortunate encounter. Humanly, it is fundamental. Without it, it is just the recruitment of someone you can replace with someone else. If it is a happy encounter, there will be ups and downs, challenges, successes, but if it's a happy personal encounter on the basis of shared ideals, a beautiful vision, in such a case, even if one has, as one certainly will, difficulties, ups and downs, these can be overcome. That's my understanding of Philippe's role – it is not at all a question of hiring. Besides, I've never used headhunters to fill this position because I do not believe in it. I think it should be people who like and appreciate each other.

Afterwards, we shall talk about other things, because we come from different backgrounds: each one will have a different point of view, with skills and experiences that are different.

→

Philippe Lamy (COO)

If you look at it factually, it is true that we have different backgrounds. Mine is really international business, there is therefore a complementarity that is evident: when you put down our paths and our specialities on paper, this becomes very clear. This does not mean that it is complementary, but that it ought to become so. What is important is how we interact with each other, therefore we work together and that goes beyond just work. I completely agree with Qiong Er to say that this is a business, but in the end it is a friendship. Even if it's a business, there is a great complicity and complicity is essential. For instance, on each subject, we both have points of view that are not the same, we therefore have to find a common point of reference, which is a point of equilibrium that is good for the company: it is not the lowest common denominator but rather the highest common denominator.

Jiang Qiong Er

At the same time, culturally, one is not so different, since Philippe, even if he is French, has worked extensively in Asia, Bangkok, China, and Chinese culture is therefore not alien to him. I am Chinese, I have lived, studied in France; I am familiar with European culture so in fact, culturally, we are not strangers. We understand each other thanks to our earlier experiences.

Philippe Lamy

Concretely, there are plenty of decisions that both of us take together, so compatibility goes way beyond mutual respect. It is a fundamental. Patrick Thomas tells the same story: when he was COO of Hermès, the idea Mr. Dumas had of the COO's job was that they should always be together. In the end, it's quite true. Today, in the twenty-first century, it may be more complicated than before but it's still true, for there is a need to share to find a perspective. It requires balance to be able to choose the best decision. For me it goes beyond the magnificent Shang Xia project: it is a story of friendship with Qiong Er and a story of admiration for her talent.

$\rightarrow$

It is also a real pleasure to no longer be alone when faced with decisions. I spent the last 15 years being boss and finding myself having to face difficult decisions alone. Even if you get used to it, is not pleasant, and suddenly, I find I'm not alone at all and it's really nice. It's a real privilege.

Jiang Qiong Er
It is important for our harmony for me to have a liking for management, at least to be able to understand it. I am not a loony artist. Loony artists exist. One cannot communicate with loony artists. So for a project to go far, one needs both this freedom of creativity, imagination, one needs passion, etc. At the same time one must be rational. For Philippe, he needs to have a bit of creativity in management, because Shang Xia is still small and new. One has therefore to innovate in management and in development. Philippe's role is not only to apply what he acquired during his past experiences, but also to use them and be creative. Both of us need to have Shang and Xia (top and bottom / up and down / logic and imagination). You need to have both at the same time to be in harmony; if he has only the Xia and I have only the Shang, we will never find this harmony because we will never understand each other. Shang and Xia are two faces that seem opposed but which are not at all. Each one of us needs both: when we have both, you will get good results.

Philippe Lamy
It is a duality: what is really nice is that in every human being there is a duality and this may cause conflict. Here, since we are two, ultimately there is no conflict: duality is not inside you; it is physically represented by two people. It becomes a debate, a discussion between two perspectives and it's really nice. When I arrived I said to myself: this is going to be new: it is even more enjoyable and fulfilling than I ever imagined.

→

What strikes me in China is that you start off by getting to know each other before actually working together. Is there a cultural dimension in your way of putting things?

Jiang Qiong Er

Historically, there have been many beautiful encounters between poets, artists, writers, among politicians, in love stories. In our culture, human encounters are important. What are the pleasures of life? It is not business. The pleasure of life is when you are happy. What makes you happy? It is to be with people you appreciate and want to be with. Happiness comes from that. If you do business with people you hate, you can make a fortune with them, but your life is miserable.

All that is basic. Even the creation of Shang Xia is a beautiful human encounter between me, Alexis Dumas and Patrick Thomas. This is not a merger or business acquisition but a happy encounter. I believe that man creates projects and successes; it is only because of them and nothing else.

So when building a project based on a beautiful human encounter it means that one builds it with people. They can adapt to many situations, if you have the same dream and the same passion. If a project is built on a commercial foundation, the environment changes, a crisis comes up and can break it easily.

It is therefore a lot more permanent. Even if some day we do other things, that beautiful human encounter will stay forever.

Philippe Lamy

I think it's Chinese but not only Chinese. It's surely not Anglo-Saxon, but in the end, it is also quite French. In France you work all the better with someone you know well. It is the Latin culture: there are great similarities between Chinese culture and Latin culture. One of the strong points of this similarity is the

$\rightarrow$

pre-eminence of the quality of work relationships. It is probably there that France and China meet.

When you look at the two cultures, there are several important points in common: the sense of family, extended family, the precedence of relationships at work, saving face. This contributes enormously to the primacy of relationships at work because when we are face to face and we say that we will trust each other, it is because there is the historical tradition of saving face. If he betrays you, he loses face.

French and Chinese cultures have a rapport with craftsmanship, culture, food that is common.

Jiang Qiong Er
It's a lifestyle.

Would you consider Shang Xia a Chinese luxury brand?

Jiang Qiong Er
In terms of quality, yes. But there still a reserve on our side, we do not use the word luxury to talk about items that are created, as what is most precious in the Shang Xia project is the time and the ardour that one brings to the project, the object and to the people who come to visit us. It is time and emotion.

Today the word luxury is used to a frazzle by everyone. What creates our "uniqueness" is time, the fact that people feel an emotion when they visit and when they set out to discover objects, craftsmen, beauty, service, stories. So we ourselves do not use the word luxury: we say that Shang Xia is a quality enterprise, an upscale enterprise; we steer clear of it, if not we fall into the run-of-the-mill luxury that is expensive and does not represent us.

Philippe Lamy
Luxury is statutory.

The word you chose earlier is very apt: it is a lifestyle brand, Shang Xia is "the contemporary Chinese art of living," luxury is part of

→

it, but in a very profound way. This is not a statutory brand: one does not stroll around with the Shang Xia tea service in the street! When you have a Shang Xia jewel, is not because it is more expensive or that it makes you into someone who displays his economic strength.

I had the privilege of meeting Jean Louis Dumas one day and talking to him; I asked him whether one could speak of Hermès as a luxury brand, and he answered, we aren't one. I asked why, he said, because on each of our items we sell, there is my name, so it is not a brand, it is a contract I have with our clients. This is striking because it means we're not in marketing but in a personal human relationship, between the head of a family business and its customers, it's at another level.

Jiang Qiong Er

We do not market either, but we offer. We offer, and when one offers one is more generous. In the contemporary Chinese art of living people do not know what they need: it is we who create the offer. It touches us, we welcome them, we are very happy to receive them, but if our offer does not touch them, it doesn't matter; they will come back some other time. It is an offer that we propose, not a marketing survey. That is more generous, more enveloping.

Philippe Lamy

I think the arrival of marketing in luxury has thrown luxury out of kilter, because when marketing arrives one switches to "manufacturer" logic. We have a factory and the goal is to sell as many pieces as possible. We then begin to do marketing, and that is how the affinity with the customer is created. For us in lifestyle, we have no factory, no industrial reasoning: we have craftsmen and the store is where we create an affinity with the customer. When a store manager decides to buy a product in the Shang Xia catalogue, he already has an idea of the customers to whom he will sell it. I think the entry of marketing in luxury has perverted it, because it has really led it astray, taking it to areas in which it

$\rightarrow$

does not belong. That's why today we are very chary of the word luxury.

Jiang Qiong Er

I give you an example of what happens in luxury boutiques: there is never a customer that sheds tears of emotion. Contrariwise, it happens regularly in ours, because people who enter our boutiques are affected and overwhelmed by emotion – by an object, a cultural artifact or an object that is utterly extraordinary.

Philippe Lamy

It happened again yesterday: a girl came for a job interview. I asked her if she had visited the boutique; she said she had not had time to do so, so I invited her to go and see it. When she returned, I asked her, "So, what do you think?" and she replied: "I wept."

Jiang Qiong Er

This is one example, but the most precious thing is when you live an intense moment that will stay in your memory. We serve tea to welcome customers. We have customers who return with their own collection of tea and they invite us to take tea together because it is a moment for sharing. Our style, our "uniqueness" is also that. That is where you find the value of Shang Xia.

You are going to open a boutique in Paris. If I take the example of tea, how you will make sure that what happens here will also happen in Paris?

Philippe Lamy

It's a real challenge. This is where we enter a phase where management becomes very important because you need the ability to duplicate all the conditions. I am convinced that in Shang Xia's history, like in all brands that commence, there is an initial phase where what is important is creation, vision. The execution is less important because there is only one store: it obviously stands out.

$\rightarrow$

The second phase is the ability to duplicate the whole.

Very concretely, in Shang Xia's service there are 3 things that are imperative. There are things that can be "schematized" and others that you cannot, which can be learned, but cannot be drawn up in a standard "service procedure."

There is:

- The philosophy of the service with its rituals – that can be schematized. Clients enter, one has to smile, serve them tea, etc. When speaking of the products one relates a story, or several, about them. That corresponds to standards, it can be charted. We can say that that is the easy part.
- Then there is a second level of service, which is how, in this schematized system, does one create a human connection, an emotion, an encounter between a client and a vendor, a visitor and a Shang Xia ambassador? Here it depends rather on the people that are selected: they should like to render service in the sense that they take pleasure in offering pleasure and making people fantasize. Here one cannot chart it, but one can still manage to recruit people who enjoy it, and who have Shang Xia deep in their soul. Often, at the end of an interview, we ask the question: "Is this person Shang Xia or not?" If the answer is no, we cannot recruit him/her, because the Shang Xia spirit is very important.
- The third level of service cannot be charted and it is not really possible to recruit people who know how it's done because it takes years of practice to achieve it: in a rapport between a client and a vendor there is a moment that is quite brief, a window, within which you can make a sale. It is very narrow, because it must happen at the time the customer is willing to talk about it: if it's too soon, you destroy his fantasy, if it's too late he will already have moved on to other things. Identifying that particular moment requires subtlety and an amazing knowledge of human psychology, also a very good power of observation. So you can only reach this stage with years of experience. It's not a question of achieving sales targets; it's

$\rightarrow$

just that if you really want that person to leave as both a client and ambassador, it must be done at the right time and in the right way.

Jiang Qiong Er
To maintain the same style of service in Paris or Beijing, when we ask people to join our team, they usually have experience in "skills." After that, it is important that they like Shang Xia and they really want to join us, not only for the sake of changing jobs. In which case Shang Xia is not the best choice. If you work in Shang Xia, you must have and share this generosity, the sensitivity of human contact: sales are secondary. Generosity is not learned: You have it or you don't. We therefore choose ambassadors who possess this generosity.

For people at the higher level, their cultural background is very important because today our customers are not the nouveau riche, but people who are really cultivated. They have knowledge about skills, craftsmanship and the history of China, even more than people who work in the boutiques. So to have a real dialogue and serve our customers, the people who work in the boutiques have this "cultural background" with regard to tea, the art of living, on materials, on craftsmen, and even poetry.

We have good timing, because in China there are people between 20 and 50 years of age who want to rediscover their cultural roots. If Shang Xia was born ten years ago it would have been too early – the market was not ready, the Chinese were not ready, nor were our current teams (they would have dreamed of a big French or Italian company). Today, after working in a French or Italian company, working in a Chinese firm, showcasing Chinese culture, is enjoyable. It is not even a job, and there is sincerity in everything. Customers are sensitive to this because they sense the authenticity, for as soon as they arrive in the boutique we share, we welcome, we offer them a nice tea. Everything comes from the heart.

$\rightarrow$

Philippe Lamy
It is for that reason that we ask the question during an interview, is that person Shang Xia or not? If she does not correspond to it, the rapport will be mechanical and real human contact will be impossible.

This is one of the main problems of service in Asia. The one the West faces is that the philosophy and rituals of service are not respected and one fights to reinstate them. But in Asia they are respected to the letter and executed in a very mechanical way. It bores one to tears.

When I entered your boutique for the first time, while chatting with your employees I realized they all had degrees and had worked in Europe, is this the case?

Philippe Lamy
Degrees are a more of a consequence: we recruit people who have a deep interest in Chinese culture, so they are educated people. We do not look especially for qualified people, but it happens that those who have an interest in Chinese culture are educated, and so they have degrees. It is true that the affinity with other cultures is important, because Shang Xia has a universal vocation and Chinese Culture easily crosses borders.

Will the salespeople in the Paris boutique be Chinese?

Jiang Qiong Er
One does not say salesperson but ambassador – it's written on their business cards. It's not important for them to have a Chinese "physique," the most important is that they are cultivated and understand Chinese culture, because the boutique is a place for sharing, dialogue and meeting, where we invite French people to discover the Chinese contemporary art of living, to experience, to share our passion. All the ambassadors, even if they are not Chinese, should appreciate Chinese culture. Because it is not limited by language or by nationality, it is universal.

$\rightarrow$

Philippe Lamy

To come back to recruitment regarding things that one cannot schematize. I have even seen an example, at the Ritz Carlton, where every employee has a small card that they always wear, which says, "We are ladies and gentlemen serving ladies and gentlemen." This does not fall under the ambit of standard procedures, or a routine or the rituals of service, and not even a philosophy. It goes much further – it is a very strong message that is constantly in their minds. I find this phrase very profound. I wondered whether we should do the same at Shang Xia – but we will find our own way of doing it. Nevertheless, it is a subtle and intelligent way of materializing the need to create a connection, emotion. The Ritz Carlton is fascinating: we recently went to their worldwide meeting in Shanghai. We saw how they work, talk to each other. The presentation was amazing. They resemble us quite a lot – they have a very informal way of speaking to each other, even if they speak business, it is not limited to that, they share values, and believe in things that are similar to this contemporary art of living. Sometimes you saw it in the small details. For instance, in the room where the meeting took place we were installed in two-seater sofas – so there were 75 sofas with two people each, with coffee tables. It changes the whole relationship. While being a part of a large group they still manage to preserve this culture.

At this point in Shang Xia's development, what conclusions would you draw?

Philippe Lamy

The deployment will take a while, after which we will refocus on the creative challenge. It's Shang and Xia: one day on top, another day at the bottom, the wheel turns, roles are switched. Jiang Qiong Er is creatively excellent and she has understood that one of the measures of creative success is economic success. According to me, there are many creative people who do not understand that. They think, to create one must be as revolutionary as possible, they want to change the world, but those who succeed

$\rightarrow$

are those who have understood that one of the gauges of the their creative capacity is economic success.

Jiang Qiong Er
Creativity should bring commercial success, after that the market will give us a new freedom to continue to innovate. One must always find a balance. We cannot abandon one or the other and we cannot look only at the financial results, otherwise one loses the value and meaning of the project.

Principles for Luxury Change Management

Populated by such well-known names as Cartier, Louis Vuitton and Armani, the luxury-brand industry will need to find new leadership and generate new talents to remain competitive in a global market. This book details what will be on the price tag for bringing such great firms into the future.

Karl Lagerfeld is renowned for his fashion designs, principally for Chanel and, since early 2010, for the Italian firm, Hogan, which is reported to be thinking strategically about selling luxury items in Asia. When *The New York Times* reported this online last September, it included a quote from the acerbic Mr Lagerfeld, made back in 2004: "I'm like a personage who's nearly unrelated to fashion."

In a business so focused on effervescent youth, the mainline luxury brands may be overlooking an obvious chink in their business armour. The reality is that in the next few years, many of those who have successfully guided such brands for decades will retire. Many are family-owned businesses face potential peril if they don't find ways to replace the brilliant business and fashion leaders who lifted them to unparalleled heights.

Four critical issues

The companies that dominate the luxury-brand industry will need to:

Replicate talent

Their challenge is to identify the competencies of the generation of executives that brought the business to its present heights. They must consider succession planning in order to avoid an undesirable cultural shift. Questions such as "Do we hire talent from outside or inside the industry?" should be addressed now. This must be accomplished without diluting the signature of the brands.

It can be done. We have seen leadership characteristics of luxury-brand executives that fall into identifiable managerial profiles such as "Visionary+Do-er/Innovator/Rational Decision Maker/Team Builder." These executives are at ease operating in different geographic regions and appreciate the cultural difference of employees and customers. They tend to switch easily between different time frames: from long-term thinking to short-term action. They do a rather amazing thing; they regularly reinvent the business while still preserving the brand's DNA. They acknowledge the central role of the retail staff, and finally, they can interact productively with the artists and designers. The trouble is, there aren't enough of these leaders to replace all the luxury-brand executives who are soon to retire.

Cultivate talent management

Creativity paired with creation is critical to a luxury brand's success; the management of creative teams and designers requires specific management skills – and managers who possess a strong independent streak. To be sure, managing at Chanel or Dior is not the same as managing a steel mill or a high-tech computer company. **Luxury-brand managers must be able to unify teams of designers who expect deference to their creative "genius," who prefer to be managed with a light touch, who rebel against corporate conformity and who, in fact, thrive on risk.** In other words, luxury-brand managers work with artists, and artists need people to manage the business details so they can use their energy, unimpeded, for creation of new lines of luxury.

Update customer service

Luxury-brand customers are different from mass-market customers. Clients of luxury firms expect shopping by appointment, the availability of a personal sales shopper, delivery of purchases and handwritten thank-you notes as part of the luxury-brand experience. This concierge-level service requires a professional career track that recognizes and rewards the importance of this role. Only in the past ten years have luxury brands have carved their niche with their retail customers. The new generation of customers also expects an exceptional online shopping experience. The website, Net-A-Porter.com (purchased in 2010 by Richemont), promises to give them just that. Maintaining this sensory-rich interactive website will require competencies and innovative approaches in retail and marketing that were probably not foreseen even five years ago. Today, however, the luxury industry is more about creating masterworks than mastering the customer experience. Developing ways to boost customer loyalty through new levels of customer relationships is central to the challenge of sustaining any luxury brand.

Hire Asian executives

Because countries such as China and India cannot be ignored by any luxury brand hoping to remain a global player, firms will need to find ways to develop executives who understand Asian preferences. And those preferences differ from country to country.

In China, for example, luxury brands are going to need to learn how to tap into local entrepreneurs, to train employees at middle and junior levels (who probably have little experience in how luxury brands operate) and to actually understand Chinese consumers and local cultural trends. Such requisites for operating in the future mean that, at the very least, luxury-brand firms will need to create "leadership duos." They will have to pair an Asian executive with a European/American business leader so that both can learn from each other while establishing the brand within a targeted part of the Asian economy.

The New York Times report cited earlier on the current interests of Karl Lagerfeld (30 September 2010) noted that the Italian firm, Hogan, was employing Lagerfeld for a line of "shoes, accessories and clothing" that would appear in 2011. Then came a telling statement: "People in Milan with direct knowledge of the situation said the collaboration was a one-time event to give a robust voice and energy to Hogan, particularly in Asia, and was not intended to become a long-lasting partnership."

The goals of Hogan, as reported, are admirable. It seems that Hogan will be using Karl Lagerfeld only as an image booster to drive sales in Asia. But the regional business also needs local talent. It is important to stress here that, for many luxury brands, the lack of Asian nationals in senior executive positions across the Asia Pacific region is a major issue for the industry. As a key player (and by far the most important growth market in the region), China has become the top priority for luxury brands – but finding management talent here to convert a luxury brand into a profitable business remains scarce.

The look of leadership

One thing a luxury brand requires is a signature "look." Passing down the look of a luxury leader to a new generation will require a period of transition. That look may not be a younger version of the current CEO. In fact, it is more likely to be a signature style recognized by everyone.

For those firms in the luxury world, or those who seek to enter that world, whoever the face of the company becomes, that person will be a worldwide brand ambassador and will need *savoir faire*, uncanny fashion intuition and, because of that, will inspire the entire organization to trust his or her sense of the future.

The next-generation CEO will possess such a clear vision of where the company should go that he or she will need to insist that every detail be executed to perfection. Domenico De Sole, the former Chairman of Gucci Group, once noted, "You can have the best strategy in the world; the difference between the excellent and the incompetent is execution, execution, execution."[1]

Finally, working with a wide range of luxury brands reveal to us that to lead successful people change issues requires to think and design a bespoke framework – specific to the brand and to its category. We have identified Ten Key Principles for Luxury Change Management, which, given our experience, can help luxury leaders and managers that face such challenges.

1. There is no "one size fits all" solution for managing change in luxury; a bespoke approach is the most appropriate
2. For each populations (managers, creative, workshop and retail) involved in the process of change, set up principles of how they are expected to behave in the system
3. Devise specific communications with each population
4. Among your key people, identify those with a great capacity for spotting and selling change issues; reward them on their "change" achievement
5. Preserve the mystery of the brand's DNA by focusing on historic "savoir faire," specific skills or cultural aspects
6. Use the change process to interview your best customers about the service they want you to deliver – and implement their requirements
7. Remember that in a Family business system, fast disruptive change is not as effective as evolving change; the time factor and heritage are critical
8. Never forget that family members' concerns about fairness, status, values and control can impact your change objectives
9. Address the emotional side in your system and work to face it on a manageable level; failure here is not a definitive mistake if you learn from it
10. Celebrate great AND small successes

We hope this book will help leaders initiate new ways of addressing the luxury business, cultivating all the brand's *talents,* to achieve the greatest success.

The Authors.

Part 1   Understanding the fundamentals of the luxury industry

1. It was fashionable and politically correct at the time to echo ancient Rome for graphics. The logo was used in printed form as an outlined (empty) font and was not changed until 1996 when it was streamlined and filled as a solid black, making it more visible in printed applications while maintaining its distinctive characteristics.
2. "A color of distinction: Soon after Tiffany & Co. was founded in 1837, a distinctive shade of blue was chosen to symbolize the company's renowned reputation for quality and craftsmanship. The color was adopted for use on Tiffany & Co. boxes, catalogues, shopping bags, brochures, as well as in advertising and other promotional materials. Over time, this lustrous color became so closely identified with Tiffany & Co. that it is today universally recognizable as the trademark Tiffany Blue. Glimpsed on a busy street or resting in the palm of a hand, Tiffany Blue® boxes and shopping bags evoke images of elegance and exclusivity, as well as nature's lush bounty – long the inspiration for Tiffany design. True to the vision of Charles Lewis Tiffany, the Tiffany® Blue Box® was to become an American icon of style and sophistication. As early as 1906, The New York Sun reported, '[Charles Lewis] Tiffany has one thing in stock that you cannot buy off him for as much money as you may offer; he will only give it to you. And that is one of his boxes. The rule of the establishment is ironclad, never to allow a box bearing the name of the firm, to be taken out of the building except with an article which has been sold by them and for which they are responsible.' The tradition of the famed Tiffany Blue Box® has endured for one essential reason: its contents are unsurpassed in quality and design." Excerpts from www.tiffany.com.
3. Source: Dowjones.com
    http://www.djindexes.com/jsp/avgDecades.jsp?decade=1895 (retrieved in 2001).
4. C. Delay (1983): Chanel solitaire, Gallimard, p. 117.
5. This means that you never will have in a luxury brand what regularly happens in a mass-market brand: A new marketing team coming in that decides to revamp the brand completely – often for purely political reasons (to show that *we* know better than our predecessors).

6. Much of the information here is taken from the extensive set of inspiring papers written by Claudia Eckert and Martin Stacey. Most are available on Martin Stacey's website: http://www.cse.dmu.ac.uk/~mstacey/pubs/papers.html (Retrieved in 2002).

7. C. Eckert and M. Stacey (2000): "Sources of inspiration: a language of design," *Design Studies*, 21.

8. Bernd H. Schmitt (1999): *Experiential Marketing*, The Free Press.

9. Interview, I-D, July 2001.

10. Lynn Hirschberg (2001): "Tom Ford, Ensuring a Place for Gucci in Hard Times," *The New York Times*, December 2.

11. "Yves Saint Laurent doesn't work like that. And he never will. The idea of him doing something just because he thinks he'd be able to sell it is crazy," recalls Clara Saint. Quoted by Alice Rawsthorne (1996).

12. "Tom Pumps Up," *W*, July 2000.

13. "Luxury in Hard Times," *The New York Times*, 2 December 2001.

14. We have complemented and adapted the framework introduced in Michel Chevalier and Gerald Mazzolovo (2008): "Luxury Brand Management: a world of privilege," John Wiley & Sons.

15. Traditional "Personal Luxury Goods" represent only 30 percent of the luxury market (the other 70 percent includes cars, wines and spirits, hospitality, food and furniture).

16. It has recently begun opening in new markets like Europe and China – in a bid to become a global brand.

17. For instance when a brand that has its own stores and wholesale operations will add figures that correspond to retail sales (in its stores) and wholesale sales to determine its turnover: this does not add up to the global retail sales of the brand, figure often given to "prove" the importance of the brand.

18. Michel Gutsatz (2002): "Luxe Populi: Managing & Developing a Luxury Brand" (unpublished).

19. It should be noted however that the cost of direct or indirect Hollywood star endorsement, which greatly contributes to them getting attention, is quite high.

20. Sara Gay Forden (2000): *The House of Gucci*, Morrow.

21. P. N. Giraud, O. Bomsel and E. Fieffé-Prévost (1995): L'industrie du luxe dans l'économie française, CERNA.

22. The theoretical basis was adapted from Olivier Bomsel (1995): L'industrie du luxe ou comment associer objets et représentations, Annales des Mines – Réalités Industrielles, Juillet – Août.

23. Luxury brands will justify their prices by having sophisticated strategies to make some of their products rare or scarce: this is what we call "organization of scarcity."

24. Roux E. (2002): Le luxe : une éthique et une esthétique indissociables, Revue des Deux Mondes, Numéro spécial: Le temps du luxe, juillet-août, 16–26.

25. Ibid.
26. "Cartier Odyssey – chapter 1" excerpts from the Press Book that presents the film project.
27. Interview on YouTube http://www.youtube.com/watch?v=-jn2ZiwxI08.
28. Djelic M.L and Gutsatz M. (2000): "Managerial Competencies for Organizational Flexibility. The Luxury Goods Industry Between Tradition and Postmodernism" in: Sanchez R., Heene A., (eds), *Research in Competence Based Management*. Stanford, Connecticut (Etats-Unis): JAI Press.
29. For instance Gucci originally is a craftsman and a manufacturer dipping its roots into the Italian system of specialized "industrial districts" (furniture in Brianza; leather in Prato; textile in Biela; silk in Como; shoes in Brenta; etc.), where small family plants subcontract for major companies like Gucci, Prada or Ermenegildo Zegna. This has allowed Gucci to rely on very efficient suppliers, which the brand controls very closely.

Part 2   Portraits and jobs in luxury

1. Source: http://www.alain-dominique-perrin.com/uk/biography/richemont _group.php.
2. During an interview with one of the authors, he excused himself to attend a Watch Committee meeting. Coming back he said: "I have to tell them what is Hermès. They presented a watch to me; you know one of those watches that have a steel case that opens when you press a button. The prototype they showed me, when you pressed the button, the case went waohh! Just fast. I told them: that is NOT Hermès. It should go wouuuh! Slowly" and he opened his hands slowly...showing exactly what the movement of the case should be.
3. Adapted from "Leadership in the Luxury Industry" – Spencer Stuart, 2009.
4. Portrait written by Claire Beaume-Brizzi.
5. With special thanks to Michel Chevalier and Gérald Mazzalovo who allowed us to use these figures from their book.
6. Courtesy of Hermès.
7. Excerpts adapted from Loïc Prigent (2005): "Signé Chanel," Arte France.
8. See www.mbandfriends.com.
9. Adapted from "The Fondation de la Haute Horlogerie – Glossary 2012 – www.fondationdelahautehorlogerie.org."
10. www.lesmainsdhermes.com / « Hearts and Crafts » in English.
11. Goery Delacôte (1996): Savoir Apprendre, les Nouvelles Méthode, Odile Jacob, Paris.

    A. Newell and H. Simon (1972): *Human Problem Solving*, Prentice Hall.

12. Philippe d'Iribarne (1989): La logique de l'honneur – Gestion des entreprises et traditions nationales, Le Seuil, Paris.
13. Adapted and designed from "The history of the Kelly bag" – So feminine co.uk.com.
14. Adapted from Marc de Ferrière le Vayer (1995): Christofle, Le Monde Editions.
15. Portrait co-written with Claire Beaume-Brizzi.
16. Toolbox we co-designed with the authors for "Luxury Retail Management," Wiley, 2012.
17. The following list is adapted from some of the criteria developped in Rob Goffee and Gareth Jones (2007): "Leading Clever People," *Harvard Business Review*.

Part 3   Case studies

1. Case study designed from US newspapers and IHT articles sources.
2. It is crucial for the old CEO, to work with the help of the external advisor on his or her new role, especially where that individual initially set up the company.
3. Before him the situation was what one Dior executive once described to one of the authors as a "ménage à trois": Whenever Galliano was unhappy with Beaufumé (the CEO), he called Bernard Arnault, the LVMH Chairman and owner.
4. Reporting the opening of Dior Homme's new flagship store in Milan, WWD (28 February 2002) says: "The startlingly modern boutique bowed last week at 14 Via Montenapoleone, next to the Dior women's unit. It is Slimane's first flagship for Dior Homme and is a surgically precise statement of Dior Homme's brand values and the designer's rigorous but seductive aesthetic. Slimane conceptualized the architectural concept with technical assistance from Architecture & Associes, the firm with which he worked on his stark, gallery like Paris atelier. Slimane oversaw all the details, from the selection of French light artist Pierre Huyghe for the fitting rooms to the playlist of electronic music from the German label Mille Plateaux/Force Tracks and such French artists as Readymade."
5. ELLE France, 25 February 2002.
6. WWD, 3 December 1998.
7. ELLE France, 25 February 2002.

Part 4   A luxury talent methodology

1. "Managerial Competencies for Organizational Flexibility. The Luxury Goods Industry Between Tradition and Postmodernism" in: Sanchez R.

and Heene A., *Research in Competence Based Management*. Stanford, Connecticut (United States): JAI Press, 2000.

2. Each subset capability, mentioned in the different tables, translates key behaviors that luxury professional already *master or have to acquire*.
3. Djelic M.L. and Gutsatz M. (2000): "Managerial Competencies for Organizational Flexibility. The Luxury Goods Industry Between Tradition and Postmodernism" in: Sanchez R. and Heene A., *Research in Competence Based Management*. Stanford, Connecticut (Etats-Unis): JAI Press.
4. Excerpts from a Franco Cologni interview in Creative Academy Website.
5. Michel Chevalier and Michel Gutsatz (2012): *Luxury Retail Management*, Wiley.
6. Adapted from Dave Ulrich and Norm Smallwood (2008): *Leadership Code*, Harvard Business Press.
7. Adapted from M. Kets de Vries (1994), "Reaping the whirlwind: Managing creative people," INSEAD working paper.
8. It was definitely the case when Bernard Arnault moved John Galliano from Givenchy to Dior one year after he was recruited – he was surely "cast" as the new Dior Creative Director while he had been "recruited" for Givenchy.
9. R. Goffee and G. Jones (2009): *Clever: Leading your Smartest, Most Creative People*, Harvard Business Press Books.
10. or discounted.

Part 5 Looking forward: luxury and China

1. Li and Fung Research Center : Revisiting the luxury market in China, March 2012.
2. "A brave new world: The climate for Chinese M & A abroad," 2010.
3. Bijun Wang and Huiyao Wang (2011): "Chinese Manufacturing Firms' Overseas Direct Investment: Patterns, motivations and challenges," in *Rising China: Global Challenges and Opportunities*, Jane Golley and Ligang Song, eds., Australia National University Press.
4. Ibid, p.100.
5. http://sumagazine.syr.edu/archive/winter04–05/features/feature2/.
6. For a complete case study see our interviews of Jiang Qiong Er, Creative Director and CEO and of Philippe Lamy, COO of Shang Xia, Page 226.
7. "Stick to your carpets," *Far Eastern Economic Review*, 5 April 2002.
8. 2010 Annual Report.
9. Tai Ping Carpets International Ltd., Interim results, June 2003.
10. James Kaplan, CEO of Tai Ping carpets, The Luxury Society, 12 November 2010 http://luxurysociety.com/articles/2010/11/james-kaplan-ceo-of-tai-ping-carpets.
11. 2010 Annual Report.

12. In an interview with the authors (May 2012).
13. Western luxury brands have in their time adopted opportunistic behaviors when they over developed licensing strategies that almost killed their brand equity.
14. A. Kriz and B.W. Keating (2010): *Business Relationships in China: lessons about deep trust*, Research Paper, University of Wollolong.
15. Zhang, J. and Ma, H. (2009): Adoption of professional management in Chinese family business: A multilevel analysis of impetuses and impediments. *Asia Pacific Journal of Management*, 26: 119–139.
16. Ji Junzhe (2010): Strategic decision-making process characteristics, Confucian values and their effects on international entry-mode decisions: a study of Chinese private firms, Univeristy of Glasgow, Ph.D.

   Confucian dynamism is a paradoxical cultural dimension including long-term orientation traits (persistence / thrift / ordering relationships by status / having a sense of shame) and short-term orientation traits (personal steadiness / protecting one's face / respect for tradition / reciprocation of favors).
17. K. Jayaraman (2009): "Doing business in China; A Risk Analysis," *Journal of Emerging Knowledge on Emerging markets*, 1(1).
18. The example of how the luxury industry previously dealt with the Japanese market is one *not* to be followed! Very few brands have had the courage like Louis Vuitton to hire a Japanese General Manager from outside the industry – who led the brand to the success we know.
19. The Economist – special China issue 2011.
20. Egon Zehnder International – Talent in Emerging markets – White Paper, 2009.
21. All quotes here come from personal communications to the authors.
22. D. A. Ready, Lynda A. Hill and J. A. Conger (2008): " Winning the race of Talent in Emerging markets," *Harvard Business Review*.
23. E. Hemmerle (2011): "Solving China's luxury talent puzzle," Heidrick & Struggles Consumer Insights.
24. This interview with Jiang Qiong Er and Philippe Lamy was done by Michel Gutsatz in Shanghai on 7 June 2012.

Conclusion: Principles for Luxury Change Management

1. At the Les Echos Conference "Luxe" in 1999.

Relevant writings and materials about the luxury sector

Luxury brand management: A world of privilege, Michel Chevalier and Gérald Mazzalovo, Wiley, 2008.

Luxury retail management: How the world's top brands provide quality products and service support, Michel Chevalier and Michel Gutsatz, Wiley, 2012.

Luxury China: Market opportunities and potential, Michel Chevalier and Pierre Xiao Lu, Wiley, 2009.

Luxe, Christian Blankaert, Le Cherche Midi, 2007.

Luxe Populi: Managing and developing a luxury brand, Michel Gutsatz (unpublished) 2002.

Le luxe: Essais sur la fabrique de l'ostentation sous la direction de Olivier Assouly, IFM Editions du Regard, 2000.

Le Luxe Eternel: De l'âge du sacré au temps des marques le débat, Gallimard, 2003.

Luxe Oblige: Vincent Bastien, Jean Noel Kapferer, Eyrolles Editions de l'Organisation, 2008. (English version: *The Luxury Strategy,* Kogan Page Ltd., 2009)

Revisiting the luxury market in China, Li and Fung Research Center, March 2012.

Selling Luxury, Robin Lent and Genevieve Tour, Wiley, 2009.

"Signé Chanel": Loïc Prigent, Arte France, 2005.

Chanel solitaire: C Delay, 1983.

Christofle: Marc de Ferrière le Vayer, Le Monde Editions, 2005.

"Sources of inspiration a language of design," C. Eckert and M. Stacey, *Design studies*, 2000.

"Tom Ford ensuring a place for Gucci in hard times," Lynn Hirsberg, *The New York Times*, 2001.

L'industrie du luxe ou comment associer objets et représentations, Olivier Bomsel Annales des Mines – Réalités Industrielles, Juillet – Août, 1995.

L'industrie du luxe dans l'économie française, P.N. Giraud, O. Bomsel and E. Fieffé-Prévost CERNA, 1995.

Le luxe: une éthique et une esthétique indissociables: Roux E., *Revue des deux mondes*, Numéro spécial: le temps du luxe, juillet-août, 2002.

The House of Gucci: Sara Gay Forden, William Morrow, 2000.

The talent Agenda: A state of the industry briefing on People and HR management, Luxury Society Report, July 2010.

The cult of the luxury brand: Inside Asia's love affair with luxury, Raha Chada and Paul Husband, Nicholas Brealey, 2006.

Marque et récits: la marque face à l'imaginaire culturel contemporain, Bruno Remaury, IFM Du regard Editions, 2004.

Bain & Company, *Luxury goods worldwide study,* 10th Edition, October 2011.

Heidrick and Struggles, "When the brand is your boss," Marika Rathle and Alessandra Brassetti, 2010.

"Managerial Competencies for Organizational Flexibility: The Luxury Goods Industry Between Tradition and Postmodernism," Djelic M.L. and Gutsatz M. (2000): in Sanchez R., Heene A., eds., *Research in Competence Based Management.* Stanford, Connecticut (Etats-Unis), JAI Press.

The changing of the golden guard: Gilles Auguste and Michel Gutsatz, *Business Strategy Review,* Spring issue, 2011.

"Leadership in the Luxury Industry: Are the rules changing?" Spencer Stuart, 2010.

"Solving China's luxury talent puzzle": E. Hemmerle, Heidrick and Struggles Consumer Insights, 2011.

Web sites

- www.michelgutsatz.com – Blog Michel Gutsatz.
- www.alain-dominique.perrin.com (official biography)
- www.mbrandfriends.com (Max Büsser web site)
- www.fnuovo.com (Frank Nuovo web site)
- www.maisonauclert.com (Marc Auclert web site)
- "The history of Kelly bag": Sofeminine.co.uk
- Worldtempus.com: Watch making Manufactures articles.
  - The watch-making factory a cultural exception
  - Tag Heuer or technology at the extreme
  - Jaeger le Coultre when passion leads to achievement
  - The HH foundation – Glossary 2012

Annual Reports and Accounts 2011

- RICHEMONT
- HERMES
- LVMH
- PPR
- COACH
- TIFFANY
- PRADA

Other relevant writings and material about leadership and talent issues

"Adoption of professional management in Chinese family business: a multilevel analysis of impetuses and impediments," *Asia Pacific Journal of Management*, Zhang, J. and Ma, H., 2009.

"Are Leaders Portable?" Boris Groysberg, Andrew N. McLean and Nithin Norhia, *Harvard Business Review*, May 2006.

"A brave new world: the climate for Chinese M&A abroad," 2010.

"Business Relationships in China: lessons about deep trust," A. Kritz and B.W. Keating, Research paper University of Wollollong, 2010.

"Business evolves, leadership endures": Leadership traits that stand the test of time, Andrea Redmond, Charles A. Tribbett III, with Bruce Kasanoff, RRA Leadership series, 2004.

"Build better bosses: a people strategy for Asia's markets," Carolyn Chan, Heidrick and Struggles, White paper, 2011.

"Building a leadership brand," Dave Ulrich and Norman Smallwood, *Harvard Business Review*, 2007.

Career Paths: *Charting courses to success for organization and their employees*, Gary W. Carter, Kevin W. Cock and David W. Dorsey, Blackwell, 2009.

CEO – The low-down on the top job, Kevin Kelley, FT Prentice Hall, 2008.

Chinese Manufacturing Firms' Overseas Direct Investment: patterns, motivations and challenges, Bijun Wang and Huiyao Wang, 2011.

Executive Intelligence: What all great leaders have, Justin Menkes, Collins, 2005.

Experiential Marketing: How to get customers to sense, feel, think, act, relate, Bernd H. Schmitt, The Free Press, 1999.

L'élan de la Sociodynamique, J.C. Fauvet, Ed Organisation, 2001.

Great People Decisions, Claudio Fernandez Araoz, Wiley, 2007.

Family Business on the Couch: A psychological perspective, Manfred F.R. Kets de Vrie and, Randel S Carlock, Wiley, 2007.

Head, Hurt and Guts: How the world's best companies develop complete leaders, David L. Dolitch, Peter C. Cairo and Stephen H. Rhinesmith, Josey Bass, 2006.

"Leading Clever People," Bob Goffee and Gareth Jones, *Harvard Business Review,* 2007.

"The five attributes of enduring family businesses," *McKinsey Quarterly,* January 2010.

The leadership code: Five rules to lead, Dave Ulrich, Nom Smallwood and Kate Sweetman, Harvard Business Press, 2008.

The leadership mystique: Leading behavior in the human enterprise, Manfred F.R. Kets de Vries, FT Prentice Hall, 2001.

"The New Leaders: Transforming the art of leadership into the science of results," Daniel Goleman, Richard Boyatsis and Annie Mc Kee, Harvard Business School Press, 2003.

"Succeeding succession," James M. Citrin and Dayton Ogden, *Harvard Business Review*, November 2010.

"Six talent dilemmas facing multinational companies in China," RRA series, 2010.

Talent 3.0: Solving the digital leadership challenge: a global perspective, Spencer Stuart, 2011

"Winning the race of talent in Emerging markets," D.A. Ready, Lynda A. Hill and J. A. Conger, *Harvard Business Review*, 2008.

"Innovation in Turbulent Times," Darell K. Rigby, Kara Gruver and James Allen, *Harvard Business Review* 2009.

"Creativity and the role of leader," Teresa M. Amabile and Mukti Khaire, *Harvard Business Review* 2008.